INTERNET ADDICTION

**Recent Titles in
Health and Medical Issues Today**

Concussions
William Paul Meehan III

Drug Resistance
Sarah E. Boslaugh

Work-Life Balance
Janice Arenofsky

The Body Size and Health Debate
Christine L. B. Selby

Obesity, Second Edition
Evelyn B. Kelly

Infertility Treatments
Janice Arenofsky

Assistive Technology for People with Disabilities
Denis K. Anson

Transgender Health Issues
Sarah Boslaugh

The Vaccine Debate
Tish Davidson

Stem Cells, Second Edition
Evelyn B. Kelly

Prescription Drug Abuse
Robert L. Bryant and Howard L. Forman

Universal Healthcare
Claudio Butticè

Genetic Testing
Sarah Boslaugh

INTERNET ADDICTION

Kathryn Vercillo

Health and Medical Issues Today

GREENWOOD
™

An Imprint of ABC-CLIO, LLC
Santa Barbara, California • Denver, Colorado

Library of Congress Cataloging in Publication Control Number: 2019917717

ISBN: 978-1-4408-6606-7 (print)
      978-1-4408-6607-4 (ebook)

24 23 22 21 20   1 2 3 4 5

This book is also available as an eBook.

Greenwood
An Imprint of ABC-CLIO, LLC

ABC-CLIO, LLC
147 Castilian Drive
Santa Barbara, California 93117
www.abc-clio.com

This book is printed on acid-free paper ∞

Manufactured in the United States of America

This book discusses treatments (including types of medication and mental health
therapies), diagnostic tests for various symptoms and mental health disorders, and
organizations. The author has made every effort to present accurate and up-to-date
information. However, the information in this book is not intended to recommend or
endorse particular treatments or organizations, or substitute for the care or medical
advice of a qualified health professional, or used to alter any medical therapy without
a medical doctor's advice. Specific situations may require specific therapeutic
approaches not included in this book. For those reasons, we recommend that readers
follow the advice of qualified health-care professionals directly involved in their
care. Readers who suspect they may have specific medical problems should consult a
physician about any suggestions made in this book.

This book is dedicated to my brother and sister, who not only are my best friends but also provide me with some of the best examples in my real life of how to put the devices down and truly engage with the life that's right in front of me.

CONTENTS

SERIES FOREWORD

Every day, the public is bombarded with information on developments in medicine and health care. Whether it is on the latest techniques in treatment or research, or on concerns over public health threats, this information directly affects the lives of people more than almost any other issue. Although there are many sources for understanding these topics—from Web sites and blogs to newspapers and magazines—students and ordinary citizens often need one resource that makes sense of the complex health and medical issues affecting their daily lives.

The *Health and Medical Issues Today* series provides just such a one-stop resource for obtaining a solid overview of the most controversial areas of health care in the twenty-first century. Each volume addresses one topic and provides a balanced summary of what is known. These volumes provide an excellent first step for students and lay people interested in understanding how health care works in our society today.

Each volume is broken into several parts to provide readers and researchers with easy access to the information they need:

Part I provides overview chapters on background information— including chapters on such areas as the historical, scientific, medical, social, and legal issues involved—that a citizen needs to intelligently understand the topic.

Part II provides capsule examinations of the most heated contemporary issues and debates, and analyzes in a balanced manner the viewpoints held by various advocates in the debates.

Part III provides case studies that show examples of the concepts discussed in the previous parts.

A selection of reference material, such as a timeline of important events, a directory of organizations, and a bibliography, serves as the best next step in learning about the topic at hand.

The *Health and Medical Issues Today* series strives to provide readers with all the information needed to begin making sense of some of the most important debates going on in the world today. The series includes volumes on such topics as stem-cell research, obesity, gene therapy, alternative medicine, organ transplantation, mental health, and more.

PREFACE

We as a society increasingly recognize that there are problems, including those that potentially cause serious harm to our brains, that come along with this new world of being constantly connected to our screens and devices. One of the problems is the risk of Internet addiction. This is a controversial label, which, as we'll see in this text, we are still learning how to define. As fast as studies come out to help us better understand the issue, technologies change and the effects they have on us change as well. It's hard to keep up, both from a consumer perspective and from a research point of view. This book is designed to help people understand what we know so far about Internet addiction.

This book is written for an undergraduate audience studying across diverse topic areas because it is an issue that will affect people in a variety of fields from education to neuroscience. This book is also of relevance and interest to the average reader who wants to learn more about what constant Internet use is doing to our minds, bodies, and social lives. Parents who are concerned about raising children in this tech-heavy world, therapists and doctors who increasingly see clients who present symptoms related to Internet addiction, and individuals who are struggling with their own use may all gain insight and information from reading this book.

The book presumes that, though some argue against it (and we do discuss that debate), there is such a thing as Internet addiction. It exists on the spectrum, and the book addresses that spectrum, but primarily it is about what happens for people who are on the side of the spectrum where full-blown addiction does occur. Throughout Part 1 of the book (Chapters 1–6), we look at the effects overuse and addiction have on the brain, the types of content that people frequently find addictive online, and the most at-risk populations. In Part 2 (Chapters 7–11), we discuss some of the more controversial aspects of the topic, including treatment options, why some people don't consider Internet addiction a true diagnosis because of the variety of complicating factors, how the Internet can also be a mental health benefit (not just a detriment), and who might bear some responsibility for addressing this issue further in the years to come.

If you've ever felt like you're spending more time than you want on your phone, your gaming system, or your social media, then this book can help you gain a solid understanding of the basics underlying this issue. Furthermore, it can get you thinking and talking about ways to maximize the benefits of the Internet, including emerging technologies like virtual reality, while mitigating the harms.

Acknowledgments

I want to thank the people who have paved the way before me with their research into this complicated twenty-first-century topic. In particular, I want to recognize the thought leaders from Silicon Valley, such as Tristan Harris (formerly of Google), who recognized that their tech companies were making choices that intentionally led users into addiction, and instead of sitting by quietly they raised the flag to make us all aware of the potential harms this could cause.

I want to thank my publishing team at ABC-CLIO for believing in the importance of this book and making it happen. In particular, thanks to my editor Maxine Taylor. I am passionate about exploring mental health issues that affect people in society today, helping to raise awareness in order to help people and destigmatize challenges. I am grateful to the publisher for also sharing this passion.

As always, this book couldn't have happened without the constant, ongoing support of my family and friends, who encourage me during the times when it feels like I don't know what I'm doing and can't get the work done to my own satisfaction.

INTRODUCTION

How often do you check your phone for text messages, emails, and social media updates? What does it feel like if you forget your phone and find yourself without it? If the power goes out and you can't access the Internet, do you struggle to figure out how to pass the time? You're not alone. The pervasiveness of the Internet in recent years offers many benefits to our society, but it's also intrusive. The very nature of the changing technology has made it so that we are all increasingly a little bit addicted to the Internet.

Internet addiction exists on a spectrum, and most of us are somewhere on that spectrum today. This book primarily covers the extreme end of the spectrum where full-blown addiction leads to serious problems in life including job loss, destruction of relationships, and comorbidity with other mental and physical health problems. It will help you understand what it is like to live with Internet addiction; how it affects individuals, families, and communities; and what options there are for treating this emerging issue.

Most of us aren't at that extreme end of the spectrum. However, it's a slippery slope. Understanding the ways in which the Internet is increasingly addictive for all people can help you take precautions in your own life in order to prevent heading down that slope yourself. Knowing the signs and risks of Internet addiction can allow you to see when someone you love might need to step back from their devices for a little bit. Most important, gaining a deeper understanding of the issue can help each of us proceed more consciously with our Internet use.

No one is suggesting giving up the Internet entirely (although some people with addiction choose to do so). In today's world, it's nearly impossible to work or socialize without some degree of Internet connectivity. That's perfectly fine. However, we can choose to use the Internet in a focused, intentional way that allows each of us to make the most of the technology instead of letting the technology get the best of us. We can recognize warnings of addiction and take appropriate steps to mitigate the harms in the lives of ourselves and our children.

Naturally, in order to understand Internet addiction, we have to define it. We'll do that in Chapter 1, looking at some of the official diagnostic criteria that various professionals use to help clients determine whether or not they're dealing with addiction. We'll also look at some ways that people can self-identify whether or not their Internet use is becoming a problem. Finally, in this chapter, we will address the important distinction between addiction and simply being creatures of habit. How do you know if it's really addiction? It's hard to tell where any one person lands on the spectrum, particularly yourself when you are deep inside of the issue, but this chapter helps gives you a better perspective on what Internet addiction really means. At the end of the book, you will also find five case studies that can help you get a more personal sense of what it is like to live with Internet addiction.

Chapter 2 digs deep into why it's a problem to have this type of addiction. Most of us are so used to the prevalence of online technology that we don't necessarily see it as a serious issue. Sure, we might have a sense that we could all benefit from a digital detox now and then. However, most of us don't bother to take one, and that suggests that we don't see the real harm at play here. Gaining a deeper understanding of how serious the issue can get for some people helps open our eyes to why it's a problem worthy of discussion, attention, concern, and treatment. We look at some of the major mental, physical, and social repercussions of Internet addiction, thickening our comprehension of why we need to address this issue sooner rather than later.

Moving on from defining Internet addiction and why it's a problem, we'll take a moment to examine the human brain as it relates to addiction. Chapter 3 lays out the science of the matter, helping set the groundwork for understanding what makes the Internet so addictive to the human brain. After we begin to get a grasp on why the brain easily becomes addicted to this medium, we will touch on the important topic of how the technology industry has exploited the brain's weaknesses specifically to generate addiction. Companies of all kinds have used what we know from both psychology and neuroscience to intentionally make the Internet more addictive. That's why so many people are affected by this issue today.

Next, we'll break down the different types of Internet addiction people commonly face. The Internet is increasingly a social tool, so Chapter 4 covers all of the forms of addiction related to people's relationships on the Internet. Social media addiction is one of the most common forms of the condition, and it comes in many forms including addiction to selfies, likes, image management, catfishing, and even cyberbullying. Many of society's issues, particularly those afflicting the young, relate directly to social media addiction. Chapter 4 also covers addictions to texting, online dating, and Internet pornography. The latter is one of the most widely studied forms of Internet addiction to date.

Although social media and the relational aspect of the Internet are highly addictive, people can become addicted to this technology in many other ways as well. Chapter 5 explores some of the most common nonrelational Internet addictions starting with online gaming. As with pornography, Internet gaming is one of the most widely studied forms of Internet addiction. In fact, it's the only form to have an official diagnosis at a professional psychiatric level. Like pornography, it straddles the line between a social/relational addiction and a solo addiction, which is why the chapter begins with this topic.

The rest of the issues in this chapter are generally solo endeavors. Compulsive Internet behavior is common, so we'll look at addictions to online gambling, stock trading, shopping, and auctions. In recent years, video streaming technology has improved dramatically, allowing us to easily develop an addiction to "binge-watching" television shows, movies, video clips, and the news. News addiction is a particularly prevalent problem emerging in society today. Finally, this chapter wraps up with a condition that you may not have heard of but might be able to relate to: cyberchondria. This is a form of hypochondria directly related to the tendency to search online for information about potential medical conditions, becoming increasingly certain that you're deathly ill because of what the Internet has to say.

If you have ever stayed up late at night on a site like WebMD, then you have a sense of what cyberchondria can feel like. You also see how easy it might be to become addicted to any behavior or content online. Virtually anyone can develop Internet addiction. However, there are certain populations that are more at risk than others, which is the topic covered in Chapter 6. We start with children and teens because their developing brains make them particularly vulnerable to the risk of Internet addiction. Then we explore a variety of other conditions and issues that can put someone at greater risk than the general population.

At this point, you might be wondering what can be done about this increasingly prevalent problem in our society. Chapter 7 answers that question as far as it relates to individuals. We look at the established and emerging treatment options available to people struggling with Internet addiction. We explore the concept of harm reduction, discuss the challenges of withdrawing from the Internet, and look at professional options including inpatient and outpatient therapy. We also explore self-help options for people who may not have a full-blown Internet addiction but who want to cut back on Internet use, go online with more intention, or utilize techniques to prevent addiction in the future.

Chapter 8 adds to the conversation begun in Chapter 7, looking at how addiction and treatment may be complicated by a variety of issues. We look at an individual's addiction in general, asking, "Would this person still have a similar addiction even without access to the Internet?" In other words, "Is the Internet really the problem or does it only exacerbate the problem?" This chapter also explores comorbidity, which is Internet addiction among people with other mental health diagnoses.

Although Chapters 7 and 8 address how to solve the problem at the individual level, this is really a societal issue. We are all increasingly reliant on the Internet for both work and play, which primes more and more people for potential addictive behavior. Chapter 9 asks the question, "If everyone is doing it, what is the problem?" More important, it looks at the benefits of the Internet, particularly as it applies to mental health. Because this book is about Internet addiction, and not just average use of the Internet, much of the content in the earlier chapters can lead you to believe that the Internet is a terrible thing putting us all at risk. This chapter helps to balance that out by looking at how the Internet can and does improve mental health generally and for specific populations. It includes asking the question, "Can the Internet help resolve the issue of Internet addiction?"

Chapter 10 takes things to the next level by addressing the increasing prevalence of Internet technology across all aspects of our lives. New and emerging technology, including smart homes and virtual reality, make it increasingly likely that Internet addiction will impact more and more people in new ways that we might not yet be able to foresee. It's important to start having the conversations about these technologies so that we can be thoughtful about how we introduce them into our lives, particularly among populations that are at-risk for addiction.

In Chapter 11, we ask the controversial and complicated question about who is responsible for helping to resolve the Internet addiction issue. Parents, schools, health professionals, government agencies, and nonprofit organizations are all working on some level to cope with the effects of Internet addiction and even to prevent it to some degree. What can each of these groups do best? Who bears what level of responsibility to take greater action? While there aren't clear-cut answers, this chapter aims to provide an overview of the options in order to start a greater conversation to resolve the issues.

By the end of the book, you should have a strong sense of what it means to have Internet addiction or to love someone who is coping with this problem. You will understand the issues affecting both individuals and communities and how, even though full-blown problematic Internet addiction isn't a widespread condition, it's a problem that affects many of us on a smaller scale. As technology advances, more people are exposed to the risk of greater addiction. By examining the treatment options, complicating factors, and big questions toward the end of the book, perhaps you yourself will begin to dream up some of the answers that can help all of us with this issue in the future.

PART I

Overview and Background Information

CHAPTER 1

What Is Internet Addiction?

DEFINING INTERNET ADDICTION

Defining Internet addiction is no simple thing. At what point does regular use go beyond habitual and into addiction? Who gets to define this issue? After all, we don't want to pathologize behavior that everyone we know, including ourselves, engages in to some degree. And yet, we're seeing signs of serious Internet addiction across all sectors of our society. There are accounts of children dying because their parents were so immersed in online gaming that they neglected to give them proper care. There are cases in which people are so addicted to staying on the Internet that they stop eating, bathing, or even going to the restroom normally—instead wearing adult diapers so that they don't ever have to leave the screen. Prolonged, nonstop online activity has led some people into full-blown psychosis, in which they develop paranoid thinking along with auditory and visual hallucinations that require inpatient treatment for weeks, or even months, to resolve. Clearly, there is such a thing as Internet addiction that goes beyond the regular person's tendency to perhaps watch one too many Netflix shows in a row or get lost in the rabbit hole of social media for longer than they prefer. So how do we define that addiction?

Let's look first at what it means to have an addiction at all. In general, addiction is defined as engaging in the compulsive use of a substance or behavior in spite of negative life consequences (which may include, but are not limited to, a negative impact on health, relationships, and finances). Addiction also has signs of withdrawal, cravings, and increased tolerance. Let's consider alcohol addiction, for example. Many people drink beer or wine on a regular basis. Historically, it was very common for people to have a "cocktail hour" each day after work. That's ongoing, regular, repetitive behavior. However, that alone doesn't mean that the person has an addiction. If the person can't stop themselves from compulsively drinking alcohol on a daily basis, then there's a big red flag that this might be addiction. If drinking every day impacts their life in a negative way, and they still can't or won't quit, then it's almost certainly addiction. If they do try to quit and experience the symptoms of alcohol withdrawal, then there's addiction at play.

As you can see, addiction exists on a spectrum. With alcohol, some people drink regularly, but it doesn't negatively impact their lives in any significant way. They can stop if they choose to do so. Sure, there might be a little bit of withdrawal symptoms, but they can manage and get through it. That's not addiction, although it clearly exists somewhere on a spectrum from "no problem" to "addicted." When the addiction begins to cause repercussions and the person is mentally or physically unable to stop consuming the alcohol, it's addiction. That framework helps us better understand what it means to have an addiction in general, which makes it easier to get a sense of what Internet addiction might be.

Internet addiction is a term for compulsive Internet use that causes some kind of hindrance to life but the person continues the behavior in spite of the negative consequences. If they do try to stop, they experience withdrawal symptoms.

It is a behavioral addiction, which is in contrast to a substance addiction. Other behavioral addictions include gambling, shopping, and overeating. To reiterate then, Internet addiction has three key components:

1. Compulsive Internet behavior (social media, gaming, pornography, online shopping, TV binges, etc.)
2. Growing tolerance (requiring more time or intensity to achieve the same pleasure) as well as withdrawal symptoms when not able to access the Internet
3. Problems caused by the addiction in one or more significant areas of a person's life (relationships, finances, health, etc.)

This latter part of the definition is the key thing to pay attention to when trying to determine if someone has an Internet addiction. Frequent use of the Internet may not itself be a problem for some people. It becomes an addiction when the person is unable to reduce or stop usage despite consequences to key areas of the person's life. It is even more clearly an addiction when the person's tolerance goes up (so they need a bigger "hit" of the Internet experience to get the same "high") and/or they have cravings and withdrawal as a result of trying to reduce Internet use.

For example, a teenager might enjoy online gaming so much that they do it every single day after school. While it might frustrate parents, it's not necessarily a problem. If they attend school, get decent grades, and have some friends outside of the online world, then there's not necessarily an addiction. Kids like video games, and that's not necessarily a sign of addiction in and of itself. But if they are staying up so late that they can't get to school, their grades are dropping, their only social life is through the game, and they refuse to eat or exercise because they don't want to get offline, then there's likely an issue. If parents take away the Internet and the child reacts with aggression or depression, which can both be reactions to withdrawal symptoms, then there's likely an addiction at play.

As you can see, addiction, including Internet addiction, isn't a clear-cut thing. Nevertheless, we can start to define it at a basic level when we look at the following criteria:

- Frequency of behavior, including whether or not that has increased: has the person started using the Internet more and more over time?
- Duration of behavior, both in individual sittings and over length of time: a person who is online for twenty-four hours nonstop likely has some level of addiction.
- Impact of Internet use on physical, psychological, emotional, spiritual, social, and financial health: what areas of life are affected and to what degree?
- What happens when the person tries—or is forced—to give up the Internet? Cravings to get back on the Internet and/or symptoms of withdrawal are strong indicators of Internet addiction.

Although this basic definition is the most important part of a diagnosis, it's worth taking a look at the history of Internet addiction to get a better sense of how to define it. It's also important to consider how the mental health and medical communities define the condition according to various diagnostic criteria.

History of Defining Internet Addiction

Children growing up today can't even imagine a world without the Internet. In fact, I recently went to a lecture attended by multiple generations interested in learning about the impact of the Stonewall riots on gay/trans history. There were people there (baby boomers) who were immersed in activist culture in the 1960s, and they shared their anecdotes with Gen Xers, millennials, and the Gen Z attendees of the talk. This talk took place in San Francisco, so a key part of the talk was exploring how the event, which happened on the East Coast, impacted activism on the West Coast. People from these older generations shared that although they had heard of Stonewall at the time of the event, it wasn't something that made a lot of waves right away in California. That's certainly not because people in California weren't touched by the issue. Gay rights was a huge issue here. Instead, it was because, frankly, it took a long time for news to make its way from one coast to the other. It took time to interview people who were there (often by very expensive phone calls or travel), write up those stories, publish them in newspapers, and then share those news stories with people across the nation. The riots happened in June, and it wasn't until October that California newspapers really seemed to make mention of them.

The millennials and Gen Zers in the audience seemed baffled by this time lag in communication. If you grew up after the Internet was a regular part of life, it's hard to understand how long it would take for news to reach people. It's challenging to think about how few places published information about an event like Stonewall, how difficult it was to access those resources, and how unlikely it was to be able to find widely differing opinions about such an event. If Stonewall happened today, it would instantly be announced on Twitter, we would see images of the event unfolding in real time on Instagram, and every news outlet, from niche bloggers to big media, would quickly be there to report on the event. In fact, it would be a completely different experience for everyone involved, and it's important to highlight that even people on the opposite coast might feel "involved" because of the ability to participate to such a high degree thanks to the Internet.

All of this is to say that the Internet has changed our world in ways both tiny and immense. Even those of us who grew up without access to the Internet tend to take it for granted that it's at our fingertips today. Most of us have some sense of what Internet addiction is, if only because our own online behavior has grown increasingly compulsive, and sometimes problematic, over time. There's a tendency then to think of Internet addiction as always kind of being a problem for some people. We may know that cell phones weren't available during the Stonewall riots, but when we picture it, we still kind of mentally think of time moving at the same pace as it did then. We know the Internet wasn't always there, but we behave and tend to think like it was. But when we look back at the history of the technology, and how it has impacted our mental health, we realize that this is really a twenty-first-century problem.

The term "Internet addiction" did begin making its way into society at the very end of the twentieth century. One of the earliest professional studies of the condition began in 1994 when Kimberly Young of the University of Pittsburgh at Bradford used anecdotal evidence of clients to gain more information about the issue. This was a three-year-long study that was eventually published in a book called *Caught in the Net*. This period, right at the end of the 1990s, marked an increase in awareness about how the Internet was more and more prevalent and might be more and more of a problem for some people.

In March 1995, a *New York Times* article appeared called "The Lure and Addiction of Life OnLine." This may be the first time in history that the term "Internet addiction disorder" was used in a major publication. The article quoted specialists in addiction and compared the issue to other behavioral addictions, including compulsive gambling, shopping, and exercise. There were not any professional criteria for diagnosing the condition. There was simply growing awareness of the fact that people were engaging in Internet behavior in increasingly addictive ways. Our best option was to look at other forms of addiction to see how Internet behavior compared to those established issues so that we could begin to understand what it might mean to be addicted to the Internet.

It's an interesting sidenote that you can quickly and effortlessly pull this article up online today. When you do, you'll see that it begins with a note or disclaimer that reads, "This is a digitized version of an article from *The Times*'s print archive, before the start of online publication in 1996." Even as people were beginning to define the problem of Internet addiction, such an established publication hadn't yet begun to offer an online version of their work. The world was changing quickly, and we were really only starting to guess at what it might mean for each of us, particularly those people prone to addictive behavior.

During this same time period, scientists began working to find a definition for Internet addiction using measurable criteria. As mentioned, they used working models of addiction already accepted in the community. They looked at both substance and behavioral addiction, because the two forms of addiction do have many similarities. They drew more heavily on information about behavioral addiction, because engaging with the Internet is a behavior (although, as we will see in Chapter 3, behavioral addiction can actually trigger chemicals in the brain in such a way that it mirrors substance addiction). Based on the criteria for addiction in general, scientists in the late 1990s determined that identifying Internet or technology addicts required the following traits:

- Compulsive behavior
- Overuse of the technology
- Problems caused by overuse, including interpersonal and health issues
- Time management challenges, particularly due to overuse of the technology
- Tolerance requiring increased use
- Withdrawal when not using the technology

In other words, a person with an Internet addiction feels compelled to frequent and increasing use of the technology despite the fact that it's causing problems in one or more areas of their life. They go online "too much," and they can't stop even though their health or relationships suffer as a direct result of the behavior. That basic definition is the definition that we've been working with since the 1990s, and it's a good working definition of what Internet addiction is. However, over the years, professionals from various fields have adapted and supplemented this definition with a more refined understanding of the condition.

The *DSM*'s Diagnosis of Internet Addiction

The *Diagnostic and Statistical Manual of Mental Disorders* (known more commonly as the *DSM*) is a guide used by psychologists and other health-care professionals in the United States to officially diagnose all mental disorders. The book, which is written by a panel of psychiatrists, is reviewed regularly, and conditions may be added or removed based on scientific evaluation and the industry's evolving understanding of humanity. The first edition was published by the American Psychological Association (APA) in 1952; it has grown about tenfold in length since then.

There are certainly pros and cons to the *DSM*. People have a lot of concerns about labeling individuals with certain conditions. One of the most well-known examples of how a *DSM* diagnosis can be pathologizing and problematic is the fact that in early editions of the book, homosexuality was considered a mental disorder, which of course today we find appalling. This reflects how the standards of psychiatry, and thus the *DSM* diagnostic labels, are naturally directly impacted by social, cultural, and medical beliefs prevalent in society at the time of the writing. In fact, it took several changes to the *DSM* to remove the entry "homosexuality" entirely. In the first edition, it was its own "disorder." Then the label was changed to "ego-dystonic homosexuality," meaning essentially that it was only a disorder if the person felt like it was a problem. A later edition subsumed homosexuality as a "problem" quietly under the larger term "sexual orientation disturbance." It wasn't until the 1980s that it was entirely removed from the *DSM* as professionals and laypeople alike began to recognize that being gay isn't a mental health problem at all.

This is all to say that the *DSM* is flawed and has been rightly criticized, but it's also the standard that mental health professionals adhere to when giving a clinical diagnosis—which may be solely for insurance purposes but can also be a means to guide treatment. So, regardless of what you think of the *DSM* and its many flaws, it's important to realize that the way we diagnose mental health disorders in America today relies heavily on the *DSM*. Moreover, each edition of the *DSM* does reflect a wide swath of the current understanding and research related to conditions impacting people in society today. Therefore, the *DSM* editions of the past clearly wouldn't have included issues of Internet addiction since the Internet wasn't even around in those early days, but as the Internet has grown in prevalence and more and more issues with it have emerged, the psychiatrists on the deciding panel of the *DSM* have had to consider whether or not the problem rises to the level of a mental health disorder.

The current edition of the *DSM*, the *DSM*-5, does not have a diagnosis specific to Internet addiction. In fact, the only behavioral addiction that is found in the *DSM* is for gambling. This shows us that what general society recognizes as a problematic behavior—such as compulsive shopping or overeating—hasn't necessarily made it into the *DSM*, yet, because there is a stringent process for editing the *DSM* in each new version and that process hasn't always caught up with the realities of the modern world. This isn't necessarily a good thing or a bad thing. It's good that it takes a long time for psychiatrists to assess a problem to determine what it really means and what the criteria would be to diagnose it. It's a good thing that we don't immediately pathologize problematic behaviors by giving them a diagnostic label.

On the other hand, a lot of the treatment options in our society require a mental health diagnosis. If there is no diagnosis for "overeating" or "Internet addiction," then it can be much harder for people facing those challenges to find affordable care to help in dealing with the reality of those issues. So, there are some good reasons for labeling a problem as a disorder in the *DSM*, but there is also a lot of caution around adding new terms.

It is worth noting that Internet addiction has sometimes been viewed as an impulse control disorder. The *DSM*-3 was the first edition of the manual that included disorders of impulse control. Those disorders included klep-tomania and pyromania. The defining feature of those disorders is that there is an impulse and the person fails to resist that impulse, despite the fact that it harms self or others. The individual struggling with impulse control will feel tension before giving into the impulse, relief while com-pleting the act, guilt after the act, and withdrawal until the tension builds, and the cycle starts over again. People attempting to quit Internet addic-tion may experience this same cycle of feelings. While the Internet didn't widely exist during the time of the *DSM*-3, if it had, then it might have fallen under the "impulse control disorder" category. That category still exists today. Therefore, a person seeking treatment might be able to work with professionals using that definition of Internet addiction even though the specific disorder of Internet addiction isn't listed in the *DSM*.

Internet addiction is a relatively new thing in our society. It has evolved rapidly with the rise and change of technology including not only comput-ers but also smartphones and other widely accessible devices from tablets to cloud-based technologies and voice-activated personal assistants like Alexa. It's no surprise that Internet addiction as a whole is not represented in the *DSM*, yet. It's just too new an issue for us to really know how to address it. That said, there is one aspect of Internet addiction that is men-tioned in the *DSM*-5, in a section recommending further study. That aspect is Internet gaming disorder.

One of the things that has to happen in order for people to widely accept a specific diagnosis with detailed criteria is that studies have to take place to determine what it means to have this illness. It takes time for those stud-ies to occur. In terms of the Internet, some behaviors are older than oth-ers. Internet gaming and online pornography are two of the oldest, most prevalent, most addictive Internet behaviors. Therefore, they are the most widely studied. It's no surprise that online gaming was the first form of the condition to receive official *DSM* attention. It has enough of a history—and the studies to support the claims—to suggest it's an issue.

Recent editions of the *DSM*, in particular, recognize the flaws inher-ent in this system of diagnosis. That's why the book has become increas-ingly broader, sometimes opting not to define a condition as a disorder but instead to recommend more study for future editions. This lends cred-ibility to the issue as a potential problem, gives professionals some ideas of what to look for in assessing people for the problem, and lends legiti-macy to additional studies into the issue. That's where we are currently at with Internet gaming disorder in the *DSM*. It's not an official diagnosis, but it's emerging as enough of a problem that the authors recommend fur-ther study.

International Classification of Diseases
on Internet Addiction

The *DSM* is the "gold standard" of diagnosis in the United States. However, people around the world are equally or more likely to turn to a similar tool: the *International Classification of Diseases* or *ICD*. This is a system maintained by the World Health Organization (WHO) to classify all different types of health issues, including those related to mental health. It's very common for *DSM* diagnoses and *ICD* diagnoses to look similar, but there are also differences between the two. If you want to fully understand a mental health issue, a good place to start is to look at the similarities and differences between how it is defined by the *DSM* and the *ICD*.

The WHO has been working with the *ICD*-10 edition since 1992. Since there weren't even studies of Internet addiction at the time, it's no surprise that it's not mentioned in that edition. The WHO does publish minor updates annually, but there hasn't been a big edition change since that time, until recently. The WHO officially accepted *ICD*-11 in May 2019, and this new edition's guidelines will go into full effect in 2022. This new edition, like the newest version of the *DSM*, includes the online gaming aspect of Internet addiction. Unlike the *DSM*, it's not "recommended for further study" but is officially included as a diagnosis.

The *ICD* says that gaming disorder is a pattern of digital or video gaming (which these days basically always takes place online) with the following problematic criteria:

- Impaired control over gaming behavior
- Giving more and more priority to gaming over other daily activities and interests
- Continuing or escalating negative consequences in life

ICD-11 is conservative in its diagnosis in that it requires symptoms to be present for at least one year. Some would suggest that six months of nonstop gaming with continued use despite problems in multiple areas of life could be considered an addiction. However, the official diagnosis suggests observation of what happens over the course of a full year before giving someone this label.

Other Diagnostic Criteria

Although the *DSM*-5 doesn't have an official diagnosis for Internet addiction and only includes a recommendation for further study of Internet gaming specifically, it is widely recognized in the medical community and the society at large that there are many people who are struggling with compulsive Internet behavior. Likewise, *ICD*-11 does have an official diagnosis, but it's limited to online gaming and doesn't include other addictive online behaviors (yet), but this WHO change is a significant indicator of increasing global awareness about problematic Internet use.

The *DSM* is used primarily in the United States and the Western world. The *ICD* is used more widely, but it's not the standard everywhere. It certainly isn't the only way that professionals in the mental health field deal with the realities of problems presented by their patients. In fact, professionals throughout the world see Internet addiction as a growing problem. And in some parts of the world, professionals do consider Internet addiction disorder to be a real (and serious) problem. China, for example, has identified Internet addiction disorder as its number one health crisis. One tool used to measure Internet addiction in Chinese adolescents is called the Chen Internet Addiction Scale (CIAS). It measures compulsive use, withdrawal, and tolerance as well as problems with time management, health, and relationships. These are all the same indicators that we would use to address behavioral addiction in the United States or Europe, but they're applied specifically to concern about Internet use (and although that includes gaming as a primary focus, it's not just about online gaming).

Kimberly Young, the psychologist who did the first major study of Internet addiction beginning in 1994, used a screening tool that asks about different criteria including being preoccupied with the Internet. It covers many of the same questions as the CIAS model, including staying on the Internet longer than planned, trying to quit Internet use, growing tolerance, and negative impacts on jobs and relationships. In addition, there are questions about mood changes, lying to others about usage, and using the Internet as a means of escape. All of these criteria are things that professionals in the mental health field may look to in order to diagnose Internet addiction problems among clients.

There are also specific tests for certain types of Internet addiction. For example, *World of Warcraft* is one of the most widely cited games related to Internet gaming addiction, and there is a free online test to check for addiction to that game specifically. The popular version of this test, available at Wowaholics.com, is adapted from the CAGE questionnaire for identifying alcohol addiction. It asks four questions, and people who have more than two "yes" answers are considered addicted. The four questions are whether you have ever (1) felt that you should cut down use, (2) been annoyed by people criticizing your game play, (3) felt bad or guilty about playing, and (4) felt like you have to play first thing in the morning to steady yourself? Arguably, this is a really limited and perhaps unscientific approach to diagnosing a *World of Warcraft* addiction. It may still be a good starting point for figuring out if you have a possible problem.

Self-Identification of a Problem Even If It Doesn't Meet Medical Criteria

An individual does not have to be officially diagnosed with a behavioral addiction to suffer the consequences of that addiction. Many people today recognize that their Internet use is problematic for them and would like to change their behavior. Whether that use rises to the level of addiction or not is less important than the desire to change.

While plenty of individuals see a potential problem, addiction is often something that people in a person's life will point out to them. Parents, spouses, and bosses may make comments about the person's frequent use. They may do so in jest, but if it happens often enough, it might be a sign that something could be wrong. If someone expresses direct and clear concern or frustration, it's at least worth taking a look at to determine whether or not there's a problem.

If you are concerned that you or someone you care about might have a problem with Internet addiction, then Kevin Roberts might be a good resource to help you identify whether or not there is an issue. Roberts is a recovering video game addict and a nationally recognized expert and author on the issue of online gaming addiction. He runs support groups to help others. According to him, someone with four or more of the following traits may have a problem with Internet addiction. This list is specifically for Internet gaming issues, but it can be used to consider whether any Internet use is becoming problematic. The traits are as follows:

- More than two hours per day of use on four or more days per week
- Changes in sleep
- Continued use despite consequences
- Cravings to use; this goes beyond simple desire and feels like a biological imperative
- Eating at the computer
- Emotional disturbance if technology is taken away
- Glorifying gaming/Internet use
- Inability to see negative consequences
- Increasing usage
- Losing track of time
- Lying about online activities
- Mood swings

- Obsessing about being online when not online
- Persistent inability to reduce use
- Physical issues
- Poor school/work performance
- Using real money to buy things inside of games/apps
- Withdrawal symptoms
- Withdrawing from others and from other interests to use

Roberts also notes that people vulnerable to addiction experience "normal" Internet usage as all encompassing. Whereas most of us feel a little boost of energy when we check social media, a person with an addiction to it will become so focused on social media that they fail to engage with important people and activities in order to attend to their online interaction. They stop thinking about other things in life because they're obsessed with the Internet. They justify their Internet use when it's obvious to others that they are making excuses for behavior that has started to cause real problems in their lives.

Roberts's list of criteria is one of the best starting places for self-identification of a problem. You can also draw from the descriptions in the *DSM* and *ICD* for some guidance. Ultimately, though, the very best place to check is your own gut. Deep inside, we always know when there is a problem. We certainly have a lot of defense mechanisms in place that allow us to hide addiction from ourselves, but somewhere inside us the compass is pointing to our true north, and if we can tap into it, then we can get a sense when things just aren't right. The ironic thing about Internet addiction is that it does a great job of distracting us and numbing us to our internal compass, so it becomes easy to avoid sensing that there's a problem. The addiction itself takes over our attention. That's why it helps to get an outside opinion, whether from a friend or from a professional, and to use that opinion to check in with yourself about whether or not there might be an issue.

Addiction versus Habit

One of the questions that come up, particularly when people self-evaluate for Internet addiction, is whether the behavior is a true addiction or merely a habit. The best way to think of this is that the behavior exists on a spectrum. A habit, when performed often enough, mindlessly, and to the detriment of the individual, is an addiction. At the opposite end of the spectrum is a habit that someone is aware of and chooses mindfully as a desired behavior. For example, brushing your teeth is a habit that most people have. Someone who brushes their teeth compulsively, fifty or more times per day, has a problem that might be called an addiction (or an impulse control disorder or an obsessive compulsive behavior). Most habits lie somewhere in the middle of the spectrum, with many behaviors leaning toward addictive in the sense that they create some kind of discomfort or problem for the individual struggling with the issue.

Related to this issue is the issue of cravings and withdrawal. There is a spectrum to consider in this area as well. Desire and wanting to engage with the Internet lie at the habit side of the spectrum. When you began to feel a need to engage, or a deeper craving, then you're moving toward addiction. When you have a craving, it feels like your survival depends on responding to the craving. This is related to withdrawal in addiction, where not using the Internet leads to deep, intensifying cravings to use.

The world is definitely changing regarding what constitutes acceptable habitual behavior with the Internet. Look at books from 2010 and earlier, and you'll see many references to the rarity of staying up all night online or checking email during a business meeting. At the time, these were not common behaviors and were warning signs of addiction. Now everyone has their phone out all of the time; it is not at all unusual for phones to be in use during meetings and dinner dates. Many people keep their phones by their bedside and not only check them first thing in the morning but also check them if they wake up in the night. In some cases, this is a habit, and it's supported by our society. In other cases, the use can become problematic, and it moves toward the addiction end of the spectrum.

It can be hard to tell when a habit has started to control us to the point that it becomes an addiction. However, you can choose to change your behavior regardless of where it lies on the spectrum. If you have a habit that you don't think is serving you, it's worth considering ways to change it. If that habit is increasingly causing you problems in work, time management, relationships, physical heath, and/or mental health and you find yourself unable to reduce usage in spite of these problems, then you are leaning more and more toward addiction. People with bad habits may be able to reduce use on their own, while people with more severe addictions may seek help for the problem.

HISTORY OF A CHANGING TECHNOLOGY

One of the things that make it really difficult to define Internet addiction today is the fact that there is a blurring of lines between all of our different forms of technology. Is it still "Internet addiction" if what you're doing compulsively is texting on your cell phone without logging on to the

Internet? What if what you're addicted to is your Fitbit that tracks health and exercise information? As fast as we can study one form of "Internet" addiction, some new potentially addictive technology pops up, and we have to figure out whether it even falls into the same category.

Defining the Technology That We Become Addicted To

Historically, cell phone addiction was studied separately from Internet addiction. Today, most cell phones do connect to the Internet. In fact, these days everything from our cars to our refrigerators are high tech, and many of them are connected online. The technology is changing faster that we can account for as we study Internet addiction.

Mark Griffiths of Nottingham Trent University prefers the term "technology addiction." He defines this as a behavioral addiction (meaning a nonsubstance addiction) that involves interaction between a human and a machine. Some people will say that this definition is too broad. Others may say that in a world where artificial intelligence (AI) is increasingly an everyday reality, it may become too difficult to even define the difference between a human and a machine. So, technology addiction may be too broad a word or it may be too narrow, but it gives us one way of encompassing the many different devices that now relate to some degree to Internet addiction.

Another phrase has been coined by Dr. Larry Rosen, a research psychologist and expert in the psychology of technology. He's the author of a book titled *iDisorder*, which is a term he uses to define an enmeshed relationship with technology. He says that user-friendly technologies create a sense of dependence, obsession, and stress that simultaneously encourages our overreliance on them while causing problems for our mental health. He specifically explores how daily use of media and technology leads to changes in the human brain's ability to process information and relate to others in the world. He considers both gadgets and websites to be culprits in an iDisorder. So, "iDisorder" is another term that we could use in place of Internet addiction to define the addiction to changing technologies related to the Internet.

"Cyberaddiction" is yet another term that is commonly used instead of "Internet addiction." This term gives many people the sense that the issue isn't limited to the Internet, per se, but instead to the behaviors associated with using cell phones, computers, and other related technologies. "Cyber" is loosely defined as things that relate to computers, virtual reality, and information technology. Therefore, it encompasses "the Internet" but it's not limited to it, making it a broader definition than Internet addiction alone.

We could debate for hours (and some people have) about the correct name for the addiction to these different devices and activities. In this book, we use the term "Internet addiction" to describe more than just addiction to the Internet but also to other technology-based activities such as Fitbit monitoring and text messaging.

Changes in the Technology

Not only has technology changed a lot in recent years, but it also keeps changing more and more frequently. Looking back across time, we can see that it took about two decades after the invention of the telephone for a majority of society to start using the device. In contrast, cell phones were introduced in 1985 and became popular ten years later (although it took another ten years for the number of cell phones to surpass the number of landlines in the United States).

Cell phone adoption was faster than that of landlines but not nearly as fast as the technologies to come. Both the World Wide Web and instant messaging needed only four years for widespread adoption and blogging about three; it took even less than that for social media to take hold. Things are changing quickly, becoming more readily available to each of us, and we may not know how to integrate the technology into our lives in a healthy way.

A few key things have changed in technology that make it potentially more addictive than ever before. We can gain some perspective on these features by looking at the evolution of video games. Think back to the first interactive home video game systems, such as Atari. Kids would gather together around the machine, and they may get very immersed in it for a time, but the activity was self-limiting. There were only a handful of games. The games were limited to a maximum of two players at a time. The goal was to "beat the game," and once you completed all of the levels of the game, it wasn't very fun to keep on playing it. In other words, kids would naturally lose interest, and because they were in a room together, they would eventually stop playing the games to do other things with each other such as kick a ball around outside.

When gaming systems went online, it was a completely different story. Computers could connect to one another, meaning that kids could sit in their own rooms, in separate homes, and compete. They would go head to head, which meant that they were competing against each other, instead of trying to "beat the game." It was no longer just "you take a turn, then I take a turn." This increased interactivity created new options for game play that pumped up adrenaline and prolonged the amount of time people would play any given game.

With the creation of massive multiplayer online role-playing games (MMORPGs), the changes were magnified. You can play with many people, at any hour of the day or night, working with teammates to compete against others. You can constantly level up; there is no "beating the game" because there is always something more to do in the fantasy world created there. This evolution from Atari is a terrific example of how our technology has gotten faster, more interactive, and more pervasive. The games are more realistic, they happen in real time, and they are much more immersive. It is much easier to lose ourselves in a twenty-first-century game than in Atari's *Donkey Kong* or *Frogger*.

We see this same trend with other devices. Social media, for example, connects us to constantly changing information from people we know and strangers all around the world. We could never have looked at a pager every few minutes throughout the day because there simply wasn't anything there to engage with, but it is not uncommon for people to check their social media accounts or look for new text messages on their phones many, many times throughout an hour.

It is almost impossible to keep up with what it means to be overusing technology to the point of addiction when the technology itself is changing so much. The 1994 Internet addiction study by Kimberly Young (who founded the Center for Internet Addiction the following year) found that people engaged in "interactive applications" were most prone to addiction. At that time, interactive meant participating in chat rooms and news groups. Engaging with other people in this way was found to be more addictive than simply "surfing the web." In the twenty-first century, the number of opportunities for interactive communication has increased dramatically. It follows that the potential for addiction has also increased.

This has developed alongside the changes in mobile technology. At one time in recent history, much attention was given to the addictive potential of computers, without as much focus on that of cell phones. The content itself was what was viewed as addictive, and the limited technology of older cell phones limited that content. Smartphones today are capable of accessing all of the content—and more, and more quickly—as twentieth-century computers. As such, studying cell phone addiction and computer addiction separately no longer makes much sense.

The advances in mobile technology also mean a change in addictive potential. When accessing the Internet meant that you had to sit at a desktop computer, you were naturally limited in how much time you could spend online. (That's not even to mention the fact that you used to have to pay per minute for Internet use, so you were financially restricted as well.) Eventually, you had to get up from the desktop and go out into the world.

(This was well before the days when Amazon delivery could instantly bring almost anything that you needed right to your doorstep.) Even when cell phones first began connecting to the Internet, they were somewhat self-limiting. The service wasn't great, so you couldn't connect everywhere, and you often paid exorbitant fees for Internet usage. Now that Internet-connected cell phones work so well, so quickly, so affordably, almost everywhere, we can easily spend all of our waking hours online.

CHAPTER 2

Why Is Internet Addiction a Problem?

Most of us use the Internet every day for a wide variety of functions. It is just a feature of life. So, what makes it a problem? Chronic Internet use of the kind that has become an addiction has a significant number of negative long-term effects, not the least of which is that research indicates that it actually changes the structure of the brain. We will look at the brain in more depth in Chapter 3, but for now let's focus on the most common problematic issues associated with Internet addiction. These are the negative effects that people experience when they have full-blown Internet addiction and that other people may experience to a lesser degree when overusing their devices.

ANXIETY

Anxiety might be the most common chronic condition experienced by people with Internet addiction. Even people who aren't truly addicted to the Internet often experience low levels of anxiety related to their devices. For example, many of us have experienced "disconnectivity anxiety," which refers to feelings of fear, stress, anger, and frustration caused by the unexpected inability to connect to our phones or the Internet. This may happen when you accidentally leave your phone at home, when traveling in areas without consistent reception, or when the power goes out for a period of time. You may begin to worry about the messages that you're missing, feel lost as to what to do with yourself during the downtime, or think that you feel the vibration of a phone alert when the phone isn't even on you. This latter condition is widely known as phantom vibration syndrome, and some studies indicate that as many as 75 percent of cell phone users have experienced it. These things might be mildly frustrating, or they might cause full-blown anxiety. It can happen even when we consciously decide to take a break from our devices. As anxiety increases, we may break our "digital fast" in order to soothe the feelings.

Disconnectivity is only one form of anxiety that people can experience due to Internet addiction. You can get anxiety when you don't get a message, such as when you text someone and they don't immediately respond (especially if you can see that they've read the message). You can get anxiety when you post a photo and people don't respond to it in the way that you want. You can get anxiety when you've commented on someone's content and then worry about how they're going to take what you've said. There are many specific triggers for anxiety on the Internet.

Anxiety is characterized by excessive worry and the feeling that you can't control your worries. The more time you spend online, the worse your anxiety may get. It may manifest in emotional or physical health symptoms including insomnia, fatigue, trouble concentrating, irritability, achiness, and restlessness. Some people develop panic attacks, which include trouble breathing, racing heart, sweating and shaking, and other physical symptoms accompanied by a feeling of dread or danger. People with Internet addiction may experience panic attacks related to specific triggers online. For example, someone might start to panic when receiving negative comments on a blog post they've just made.

There also might be a more widespread feeling of generalized anxiety in our society related to the changes that technology has placed on our social norms and the fact that we don't have clear etiquette for those changes. Professor and author Jarice Hanson suggests that technology is causing our lives to change so much, and so quickly, that none of us are certain what the new social norms are surrounding our behavior, particularly as it relates to use of technology. Consider, for example, that children today might take offense to a text message sent by a parent that includes punctuation; punctuation is considered aggressive to this younger generation, something that older folks might not be aware of. So, when a parent discovers this, they may start to get anxiety about how to handle the next text message to their child. How many times have you had to correct a misunderstanding because what was said online or through text was taken the wrong way? With so many underlying issues affecting our society, it's hard not to feel some anxiety when engaging on the Internet.

We may also feel like technology is taking over our lives, and we want to return to a "simpler time," but we also feel like there's no turning back from the onslaught of gadgets. All of this leads to chronic anxiety related to an inability to adjust to a rapidly changing world. This can manifest in anxiety triggered by device updates that change things around, trying to learn a new app, or otherwise engaging in a new activity that feels like one more overwhelming thing that you have to learn.

Anxiety is arguably increasing year upon year in our society. In 2017, the American Psychiatric Association (APA) found that two-thirds of those polled were either somewhat or extremely anxious specifically about health and safety and at least one-third were just anxious in general. The following year, the APA repeated the study, and results indicated that anxiety had already increased by 5 percent. Of all those studied, millennials were the ones most likely to report anxiety. Of course, there could be many different causes for this increase in anxiety. However, we can't ignore the likelihood that Internet connectivity could be one major cause. This is further supported by the fact that studies show that anxiety is more common in wealthy countries, which, of course, are also the most Internet connected.

People with Internet addiction are highly likely to suffer from anxiety. It can often be a chicken-and-egg situation because people with anxiety are also at risk of developing Internet addiction. The addiction is a form of escape that can seem to help soothe the symptoms of anxiety. However, the behavior worsens the anxiety, requiring more need for soothing. Regardless of which came first—the anxiety or the addiction—they reinforce each other.

Chronic Sleep Deprivation

Anxiety might be the most prevalent problem facing people with Internet addiction. But chronic sleep deprivation might be the most problematic of all. Sleep is critical to mental and physical well-being, and yet a large portion of the population today fails to get enough sleep. Screen time at night, including alerts throughout the night, is a primary contributor to this problem.

Although losing sleep to screen time is one reason for sleep deprivation due to tech, it's not the only one. More insidious is the difficulty or inability to sleep because prolonged use of devices has left your brain too awake. This especially happens in gaming, last-minute auction bidding, and other Internet behaviors that increase adrenaline and initiate the fight-or-flight response in the body. This reaction gets the body pumping, making it difficult to fall asleep because you have a hyperaroused nervous system. It's like trying to fall asleep after watching a really scary movie.

It gets worse if you keep those stress response levels high over a period of time, which is not what was intended for the body to do. Over time, a steadily high level of adrenaline can lead to symptoms similar to that seen in bipolar mania—rapid speech and extreme excitability followed by a crash into depression that is often accompanied by sleep loss. So, someone with an Internet addiction to adrenaline-increasing activities such as gaming negatively trains their brain to stay in stress mode, leading to a variety of different issues, not the least of which is trouble sleeping.

Although those activities are the most problematic, any online use, particularly later in the day, may affect sleep. The blue light emitted from our gadgets has been shown to disrupt our sleep cycles. It can change our circadian rhythm, throw off our melatonin, and make it hard for the body to fall asleep at night. The later you use the devices in the day, the more likely it is to affect your sleep.

Sleep problems become a vicious cycle. People give up sleep to be online, and this leads to reduced ability to make good decisions, so they are even more likely to give up sleep even as they need it more. And sleep problems lead to all sorts of other problems including mood changes, trouble concentrating, problems with memory, difficulty completing tasks at school and work, and myriad physical health issues.

LONELINESS AND DIFFICULTY WITH IN-PERSON RELATIONSHIPS

Although people have an increasingly large number of "friends" (or "fans" or "followers") through social media, the number and quality of face-to-face interpersonal relationships have decreased as technology has risen. People with Internet addiction often find it difficult to interact with people in real life, substituting online relationships for real ones.

Sherry Turkle, a somewhat controversial expert in the psychology of technology, describes this phenomenon well in her book *Alone Together*, which relates her findings of studies of the social use of robots. She explains that robots were once considered to be "better than nothing." For example, if an elderly person has to be home alone all day, it is better to have an interactive robot than to have nothing to interact with at all. However, as time has gone on, and technology has invaded every part of our society, many people are now experiencing robots as "better than everything." The elderly person now might rather have the unfailing, consistent response from a programmed robot than to be forced to engage with the complicated behavior and emotions of real-life family members.

Relationships based on technology are naturally one-sided. This is true even in cases where it might seem like you're interacting with others—through social media, email, text messages, gaming guilds, and the like. Although there is technically another person on the other side of that screen, much of what we read into their messages happens in our own minds. We can't see their body language, experience their immediate response, or deal with them through honest, authentic interaction. Therefore, we fill in the blanks in our own minds. We are mostly just having a relationship with ourselves and our own projections.

This isn't always the case. Some people are actually able to enhance the authenticity and depth of their in-person connections by addressing challenging conversations online first, where they may have more time to give a thoughtful response, and then bringing the conversation into the real world. However, that's increasingly rare. More and more often, people use online communication to avoid depth while still maintaining a feeling of connectedness to others.

This is a self-reinforcing behavior; the more time you spend focused on online relationships, the more difficult it is to interact with people in the "real world" and the more likely the person will ramp up their online activity in response. We seek to stave off the feelings of loneliness by busying the brain with more pseudointeractions, at the expense of authentic, but messy, connections.

In cases of Internet addiction, there may be a desire to be alone in order to keep the addiction secret. People addicted to online shopping or pornography may spend more and more time home alone to engage in the behavior. They may feel intruded upon when others enter their space, and they may feel irritation or anger when the "real world" interrupts their online activities. This desire for alone time feeds into the loneliness.

Loneliness leads to more loneliness. Johann Hari, writing about disconnection in society, says that the longer we experience loneliness, the more we tend to socially shut down and the more likely we are to become suspicious of activities that would break the loneliness. We get wrapped up in our own minds, and we become hypervigilant toward others intruding on our mental space. He suggests that there's a biological imperative at work here; being alone, we sense that nobody is looking out for us, so we start to constantly look out for threats from others. In other words, what we desperately need is to connect with others to break the loneliness, but the loneliness itself causes us to fear others to the point that we don't want to connect. The more disconnected we become, the more we engage in behavior that disconnects us further.

The Internet can reinforce this loneliness. On the one hand, we may replace real-life connections with watered-down online versions to soothe some of that loneliness. On the other hand, we may subconsciously seek out the kind of online activity that confirms our worst suspicions about people. For example, we may begin to binge-watch online episodes of true crime, seeing evil lurking in every corner. Or we may engage in negative, destructive, back-and-forth social media exchanges that fuel our beliefs that people are out to get us or that no one understands us.

Loneliness is not just an emotional issue; it can also have physical health consequences. Johann Hari reports on research that has found that feeling lonely increases your cortisol levels. Acute loneliness can cause you as much of a stress response as getting physically attacked by someone can. Prolonged stress in the body leads to many different health issues.

Loneliness is an increasingly widespread problem. Recently, many health professionals are even naming it as an epidemic. Studies have shown that many people don't feel like they have even one close friend, that loneliness is increasing rapidly over time, and that it leads to a large number of other problems for individuals and society as a whole. People with Internet addiction frequently experience loneliness, and the Internet usually only makes it worse over time. This isn't to say that it can't offer some sense of connection for isolated people, a benefit we'll look at in Chapter 9, but it is more often a problem and is a negative effect for those who do develop addiction.

PROBLEMS ASSOCIATED WITH A SEDENTARY LIFESTYLE

As we have come to spend more and more time on our devices, we have started to spend less time on physical activity. Kids who used to spend time together at parks, or even at least walking around the mall, are now "gathering" through the screen. A sedentary lifestyle often causes fatigue and may result in obesity, the latter of which is correlated with a large number of health problems including heart disease and diabetes.

Obesity isn't just a result of the lack of exercise, either, but may also be caused or worsened by certain online activities. Dr. Doan, an MD with a PhD in neuroscience, and a recovered video game addict himself, explains in his interview with Nicholas Kardaras for the book *Glow Kids* that Internet and gaming activity can alter cortisol levels, which can lead to problems with obesity. He explains that extra cortisol dysregulates the hypothalamic pituitary adrenal (HPA) axis, and this dysregulation can lead to weight gain. So, if you're sitting on the Internet, you are gaining weight not only because of lack of exercise but also because the Internet activities themselves are making you fat.

Obesity isn't the only health issue associated with a sedentary lifestyle. Additional issues include the following:

- Hormonal imbalances
- Increased inflammation
- Mental health issues including depression
- Muscle atrophy
- Problems with blood circulation leading to various heart health issues
- Reduced immune system leading to various illnesses including higher risk of certain cancers
- Weakened bones including risk of osteoporosis

An excessively sedentary lifestyle can lead to physical and mental health problems that actually put people at risk for early death. Therefore, those with an Internet addiction that leads to increasing sedentary behavior are facing some potentially serious consequences.

OTHER COMMON PHYSICAL HEALTH ISSUES

Even people who remain active are at risk of health issues from the chronic use of devices. Many different parts of our bodies can experience aches and pains not only as a result of sitting at the computer but also because of the nature of the repetitive activities that we engage in there.

Staring at a screen all day leads to eye strain. Poor posture while using laptops, desktop computers, and handheld devices creates back pain and other aches in the body. Near-constant typing and swiping can lead to repetitive stress injuries including carpal tunnel syndrome. People with Internet addiction will continue to use their devices despite the pain.

For example, Kevin Roberts has shared his own story of how excessive gaming caused him to experience lower back pain. He ignored the initial pain, upon which he began to experience a shooting pain down his leg that was so bad that it limited his mobility. At the same time, he started getting pain in his right wrist, the one that clicked constantly on the computer mouse. Instead of taking a break, he started wearing a wrist guard so that he could continue putting that strain on his body. His addiction caused him to ignore his health issues in favor of staying online.

Dr. Dean Fisherman, a chiropractor in Florida, created the term "text neck" to describe pain in the neck, shoulders, and back associated with poor posture due to compulsive text messaging. He first called it "forward head posture," but the term "text neck" stuck, and he opened the text neck Institute. It was intended to treat mostly teenagers, but these days people of all ages are experiencing text neck.

Another similar term that people have used is "texting thumb." The term is used to describe a repetitive stress injury that typically results in pain at the base of thumb without anything broken, torn, or necessarily even inflamed in the area. The problem has been going on as long as we've had devices; in early decades it was called Blackberry thumb and Nintendo thumb, and it is comparable to "writer's cramp" from the days when people actually wrote longhand with pens. Today it is caused by the variety of things we do on our phones including not just texting but also swiping and scrolling.

People who spend significant amounts of time on their devices, especially those engaging in prolonged hours of gaming, often have an increased level of adrenaline. The body was designed to experience this fight-or-flight hormone for only short bursts of time in order to get us out of dangerous situations. Getting that adrenaline rush without ever moving around can cause a variety of problems, including physical ones; even very young people may get hemorrhoids as a result.

More important, keeping stress levels elevated for so long creates a wide range of different issues in the body. The constant adrenaline rush leads to high blood pressure and high cholesterol. Stress can decrease thyroid function, insulin production, sex hormones, and growth hormones.

As mentioned before, many Internet activities lead to extra cortisol, which dysregulates the HPA axis. This not only leads to weight gain but also causes hormonal issues. Adults spending too much time online may suddenly find themselves with adult acne. Infection can become more common as well. Your whole body gets thrown out of whack, and there is no telling what physical conditions may ensue as a result.

People struggling with an Internet addiction may experience a variety of other health issues that they don't necessarily immediately recognize as linked to their Internet use. Professionals in the medical field would do well to become increasingly aware of these potential problems so that they can help identify Internet overuse as a possible cause.

FEELING LOSS OF CONTROL OVER LIFE

One of the vaguer, but very distressing, feelings that people report with Internet addiction is a growing sense that they are losing control over their own lives. Some of this comes from the addictive behavior itself; they want to stop or reduce use but feel unable to do so, which leads to a sense of having no control over the self. As with any addict, Internet addicts may tell themselves again and again that they'll "stop using tomorrow," and then when tomorrow comes and they turn the Internet on again, they feel guilt, shame, and a spiraling loss of control.

Often Internet use leads to a sense of control in the moment, which can reinforce this feeling. Playing a game in which you are skilled gives you a sense of mastery and control. Perfecting your image on social media makes you feel like you have control over how others see you through that channel. An addict may engage in these behaviors with increasing frequency to avoid the discomfort of not feeling in control in "real life." The more time spent online, the less control one feels in the real world.

Additionally, out there in the real world, there may be the feeling that you have to "keep up with the Joneses" in terms of technology. The long lines outside of the Apple store for the latest iPhone are just one example. If you don't have the newest app, know the latest news sourced from online, or have access to the newest device, you may feel inferior. Trying to keep up increases that feeling that you have no control over where life is going.

The addict spends more and more time online in an effort to "keep up," but it's absolutely impossible when so much new information flies at you every second of the day. On YouTube alone, people upload more than five hundred hours of new content per minute. You could watch YouTube every minute of every day and never catch up. The addict who feels lost if they don't know all of the latest stuff is never going to catch up; trying to only makes the feeling worse.

DEPRESSION, ANHEDONIA, AND INCREASED RISK OF SUICIDE

Depression is a widespread problem in our society, and it's even worse for people with Internet addiction. The National Institute of Mental Health estimates that more than 6 percent, or 16.2 million, of the adults in the United States have had at least one major depressive episode. The problem affects more females than males and is most common among young adults aged eighteen to twenty-five. Of the adults afflicted, more than ten million had severe impairment due to their depression. The number is even higher for teens; more than three million U.S. teens aged twelve to seventeen have experienced major depression, which is more than 12 percent of the teens in the country. More than two million had serious impairment. Girls are more than three times as likely as boys to experience depression.

Depression and suicide aren't inextricably linked, but there's a strong correlation between the two. Suicide rates have climbed steadily in the United States in recent years. The Centers for Disease Control reports that the suicide rate increased by 24 percent between 1999 and 2014. The rate increased steadily between 1999 and 2006, and then the rate doubled after that. It may be no coincidence that the steady rise corresponds to the timing of computers and cell phones entering mainstream culture; the later years of even more rapid increase corresponds with increased prevalence of cell phones and the early days of social media.

Numerous studies have been done exploring the link between Internet use and depression. Facebook-linked depression has been a particular area of study interest. A 2014 study called "Facebook's Emotional Consequences" found that people expect to feel better after using Facebook, and yet they typically don't find it meaningful and end up feeling bad about using it so much. Its addictive nature leads us to continue using in spite of this feeling. One reason we do this is related to the way that it affects dopamine levels in the brain, something we'll look at in more depth in Chapter 3. Essentially, each time that we check our email, texts, or social media, we get a little dopamine hit, which feels really good. Our brains experience euphoric recall; they remember that this behavior caused the dopamine to rise. As a result, we continue to predict that engaging in the same addictive behavior will produce that feeling, even though we are no longer satisfied by the behavior. It's a problem called affective forecasting error; we think we'll feel good, then we don't, and that feels especially bad.

There are many reasons that Internet addiction is correlated with depression. The brain chemistry is one of them. Another is social comparison, a problem particularly linked with social media use. A 2015 University of Houston study conducted by Mai-Ly Steers specifically found that Facebook use increases the frequency of users comparing themselves to others, which in turn leads to depression. Think about it; how many times has it seemed like everyone else on social media is doing better than you are and how has that made you feel? Even if you don't struggle with an Internet addiction, the experience can have negative consequences on self-esteem and mood. If you do have an Internet addiction, the consequences are worse.

The problem is exacerbated when we experience negative online interactions, such as cyberbullying or rude comments. No matter how many positive things are in our social media feeds, we are drawn to focus on the negative. That's because negative feedback pings a specific part of the brain that seems to strike us more powerfully than positive interaction does. With so many frequent opportunities for that negative feedback, it's no wonder that social media can lead us to feel badly about ourselves. This can become, or can worsen, depression.

Before there was Facebook, the big social media giant was MySpace, and it, too, was studied for links with depression. One study conducted through the Victoria University of Wellington in New Zealand discovered that one in six MySpace users were at risk for depression and even suicide. These people were expressing negative thoughts through the site. The study wasn't complete enough to know whether MySpace itself was causing any depression or if it simply served as a place for people who were already depressed to express those thoughts, but it was an important early study on the link between depression and users of social media.

Sharing our feelings of depression online can have both positive and negative effects. For some people, opening up about depression reduces the stigma of the condition. A positive response from the online community, combined with support, can help people rebuild self-esteem, seek treatment, and take steps toward healing from depression. On the other hand, a negative response can cause immeasurable detriment. Furthermore, one can get trapped in the cycle of negative commentary online; in depression, the mind ruminates on the negative, and some people use social media as a space to ruminate out loud. Others may join in; they say that misery loves company after all. The result is more rumination, which frequently exacerbates depression symptoms.

Some researchers have suggested that generations growing up with constant online access are more likely to experience levels of depression, although it will take time for studies to confirm or debunk this theory. One interesting study highlighted by Nicholas Kardaras was a two-decade longitudinal study completed by the German Psychological Association and the University of Tubingen, in which it was found that we as a group are steadily losing our increasing sensory awareness, at a rate of about 1 percent per year. The more stimulation we get, the more we lose attention to it. This study ended in 1980, long before the excessive stimulation of pervasive gadgets always at our fingertips. Kardaras links this with a term he uses, called "digitally induced adolescent malaise"; we all feel duller because of this overstimulation. While the result isn't necessarily clinical depression, it can produce many of the same symptoms as depression.

Dr. Dimitri Christakis describes the same phenomenon in the world of highly stimulating video games. He posits that a growing person's brain can get habituated to the quick responses and high levels of alertness that are necessary to excel at the game and that keeping the brain at that pace can lead the youth to feel like the nongaming world is understimulating, underwhelming, and possibly even depressing.

One thing that is important to consider is whether an individual experiences depression first or the addiction first. In some cases, depression itself can lead to excessive, addictive use of the Internet; the opposite can also be true. It's a self-reinforcing cycle. In Part 2 of this book, we'll look more closely at comorbidity and the challenge of deciphering which issue came first. As we can already see in this chapter, many of the issues associated with Internet addiction are chicken-and-egg situations that can be hard to parse out because of the constant use of the Internet in today's society.

For now, let's look at the reasons that Internet addiction is correlated with depression. We've already discussed brain changes as well as a negative self-image caused by making social comparisons. As we know, Internet addiction also leads to sleep problems, and disrupted sleep can be a factor in depression. Exposure to negative content is also a depression risk factor; whether it's violence, frustrating news commentary, or negative body image, the content we see online can contribute to an increasingly hopeless view of the world. Finally, there is a strong link between Internet addiction and loneliness as well as a link between loneliness and depression. Each problem reinforces the other, exacerbating the risk of depression among people with Internet addiction.

PROBLEMS WITH WORK OR SCHOOL PERFORMANCE

So far, the consequences of Internet addiction that we've discussed may be experienced to some degree by anyone using the Internet. Now, let's talk about a specific criterion of addiction. Internet addiction means that you continue use despite negative consequences. So, what consequences may those be? The biggest may be a failure to meet responsibilities. Students may fail out of school, while adults may experience job loss and therefore debt and other financial consequences due to excessive Internet use.

One reason for this is that it becomes "easier" to simply stay online. The longer you're online, the harder it can feel to go deal with the real world. Interacting with people through social media means that you don't have to deal face-to-face with their criticisms, demands, or emotions; most of the interaction happens in your own mind through interpreting what they've written, and you can always turn the device off (or switch to a different online activity) if you really don't want to deal with them.

Additionally, Internet usage often allows us to experience mastery that isn't as easy to come by in daily life. For example, it is easier to level up in a video game than to get a promotion at work. Even if you fail in the game, you simply have to restart, whereas failing at a job means that you have to process the experience and work through it before moving forward again.

All of this can lead "real life" to feel too hard in comparison with life online. The longer you spend online, the more likely you are to have reduced skills in interacting with others, coping with failure, dealing with situations that require tact and patience, and so on. Furthermore, Internet addiction frequently leads to elevated stress levels and more impulsive responses, which in turn can lead to behavior, such as aggression, that isn't taken well in school or the workplace. Staying up late to engage with the Internet causes sleep disruption that makes it difficult to get up in the morning to get things done.

All of this leads to a tendency to skip class or to stay home from work. It means showing up late to important events and meeting, if you show up at all. It means that when you do show up, you feel uncomfortable and aren't a team player. Students may fail classes, or they may squeak by but be unable to get college recommendations from teachers. Adults may get demoted or fired or find it difficult to seek new gainful employment. Instead, they get online to stop feeling the bad feeling, and this worsens the situation.

ISSUES WITH TIME

Being late is just one time-related issue that can become a problem in Internet addiction. It is also possible to completely lose sense of time. Of course, this further impinges on your life when it comes to work or school, and it also impacts your social relationships. Worse, it can cause a distortion in your sense of reality, since the daily world is structured around time.

This issue has been most closely studied in relationship to online gaming addictions. Jarice Hanson writes, for example, "Games can be dysfunctional . . . when they offer a sense of time and space that is so different from reality that the user loses control of how long he or she plays a game." The game's sense of time is different from real-life time, and addicted users get confused.

This same author goes further to say that the way we view time in a digital world may have social consequences beyond yet what we can currently understand, noting that when you look at a clock face, you can see time passing, whereas when you look at a digital clock, you can see only that moment in time. This leaves us feeling disconnected from any sort of history. The immediacy of the news cycle may exacerbate this as well. Everything is made to feel so important in the moment that we are losing our grasp on the fact that this moment is just one blip in the big arc of history. Internet addiction makes it feel like right now is the only thing that matters.

Technology is now moving so much faster than humans can move. Everything online is happening in "real time," and this is actually beyond the processing time that our brains require to keep up. This results in a feeling like we're never going to catch up. It leaves most of us wanting "more time." We feel constantly rushed, under the pressure of such a fast pace, and this makes us impatient and aggressive. The addict has no sense of patience because they have no sense of time.

PROBLEMS ASSOCIATED WITH BRAIN CHANGES

As we'll discuss in more detail in Chapter 3, behavioral addiction including Internet addiction causes structural changes to the brain. This can result in many and varied issues including the loss of willpower, decreased attention span, a lack of long-term goals, risk-taking behavior, and memory loss. Larry Rosen reports that people who are online ten or more hours per day, which is very common in Internet addiction (and increasingly common among regular users), have a significantly smaller amount of gray matter than people who spend two hours or less online daily.

We outsource a lot of our memory now—knowing that we can access all information on our devices at any time. However, memory is use-it-or-lose-it. Memory exercises strengthen the brain and increase our gray matter. Repetitive passive activities including Internet use may deplete the gray matter. The addict is at risk of losing their memory.

We learn best when focused and paying attention to what we want to remember, which isn't done as easily if we are multitasking. We tend to try to multitask with the Internet, either by using multiple devices/screens at once or by using the Internet while doing other things in the real world. What we call multitasking is really more likely to be "switchtasking"— moving our focus from one thing to the other and back again. Research indicates that it takes a significant amount of time to be able to refocus and attend again to the new task. More than this, there are long-term impacts of frequent switchtasking; the brain gets so used to distraction that it can't settle down to focus, and this leads to ongoing problems with concentration. Multitasking has also been correlated with a decreased ability to identify human emotions. The Internet addict is at risk of decreased concentration and an inability to connect emotionally to others.

This doesn't necessarily mean that humans can't handle distractions. Rather, we need to have a balance between distractions and focus, and people with Internet addiction tend to be very imbalanced in this area. An important thing to understand is that we have two types of attention: top-down and bottom-up. When we attend to something with our top-down attention, the experience is one of focus. We set goals and direct where our attention will go in order to meet those goals. In contrast, bottom-up attention is when something distracts us; the constant alerts from phones and computers are bottom-up attention grabbers that, when not balanced with top-down attention, can lead to decreased attention in our lives overall.

All of this occurs as changes in the brain occur. The brain also changes in ways that increase risk-taking behavior and decrease impulse control. When we have an addiction to the Internet, we can't pull ourselves away from it, no matter how dangerous it may be to focus on a device. We hear the ping of the cell phone while we're driving, letting us know that we have a text message, and we take our eyes off of the road to see what it says, although we know how dangerous this can be. The urge to attend to the device overrules our ability to think rationally about the risk. The more time we spend on Internet-addicted activities, the more it affects our brain and the more likely we are to take such risks.

Relationship Problems

Internet addiction can lead to problems in all of our relationships, due largely to how the addict treats the people in their life but also to the changing relational behavior of someone who spends the majority of their time in a virtual world.

There are several extreme cases of people being so wrapped up in their virtual worlds that it causes devastating impact to others, especially children. One well-known case is that of an Arkansas woman and her boyfriend who were so focused on playing the online game *EverQuest* that they forgot their three-year-old child in the car and the child died. Less extreme, but more common, are examples of parents distracted by Internet use in ways that can be devastating to the parent-child relationship. A parent may play online games with their kids as a way to bond but then become frustrated and angry when the child can't "keep up" in a game, eroding the relationship that they are attempting to build.

One very serious potential problem that hasn't yet been sufficiently studied is the prevalence of infants who are not getting their much-needed eye contact with their mom (or the primary caregivers) because she is busy on her phone or computer while breastfeeding. That bonding time is critical to feelings of security in the world. It forms our first attachments, which imprint on us and affect all of our future relationships. We simply don't know what it's doing to an entire generation that might not be experiencing that bonding to the degree kids did in the past. Toddlers and older children are also lacking in parents' attention because that attention is divided between devices. What is this doing to our ability to form relationships? We don't know, but it might not be good.

Something we do know is that people with full-blown Internet addiction will often choose to engage with their devices instead of with the people in their everyday lives. This leads to hurt feelings, communication problems, and the potential for more serious long-term consequences in our relationships. People who are wrapped up in an online activity may become irritable with those who interrupt them; they get snappish and angry when parents, children, and spouses want their attention. At the extreme end, this leads to things like "gaming widows"—partners (of any gender and orientation) who feel like they are living as single parents because their spouses spend more time gaming than being with their families, a situation that has led some to divorce. There are support groups for loved ones of people with Internet addiction to help them with feelings of frustration, abandonment, disappointment, hurt, and anger.

One of the specific behaviors of Internet addiction that can devastate relationships is lying. Teens lie about the frequency of their use as well as the content that they engage with online. While some of this is normal as teens learn to differentiate from their family units and become individuals, it can lead to (or point to) problems in the ongoing trust in the parent-child relationship.

Partners/spouses also lie to one another about their usage; this is typically more about content than frequency. Lying about who you're contacting online and the information exchanged in the online relationship can be symptomatic of a problem in the relationship but can in turn also lead to relationship problems. Lying about, or being secretive around, Internet use provokes an increase in jealousy and a breakdown in trust. Partners may also lie about financial issues related to online gambling and shopping activity. In general, it is much easier to lie about behavioral addictions, like problems with Internet usage, than it is to lie about substance addictions, and the lying can eat away at a relationship for a long time before it is addressed. Sometimes the relationship cannot be repaired.

In general, we as a society often fail to give enough attention to the people whom we are face to face with because instead of communicating with them, we are looking at our devices. How many times have you been speaking with someone and their engagement dropped as they glanced at a phone screen? Our relationships are built in large part on our nonverbal communication, showing other people that we are listening and that we care about them through the attention we give them as they speak. People may think that they can glance surreptitiously at their phone and not interrupt the flow of face-to-face conversations, but the reality is that they are often responding without actually listening and truly communicating. The relationship becomes shallow and transactional rather than deep and relational.

There is also the problem that the more we engage with online relationships, the less inclined we may be to engage in face-to-face social interaction at all. This relates to the aforementioned problem of loneliness but is worth repeating here, because it's a relationship problem caused or exacerbated by Internet addiction. People with an addiction to the Internet may stop connecting with people in the real world, skip face-to-face interactions, develop social phobia, and simply stop "showing up" for their friends and family. This clearly creates a negative impact on the relationships.

WITHDRAWAL SYMPTOMS AND TOLERANCE

The problem isn't just in the use of the technology but can also come when we try not to use the technology. As an addiction, it can lead to withdrawal symptoms such as craving and anxiety. If you've ever accidentally left your phone at home when going out, you might have felt some of those feelings—anxiety, wondering what you're missing, reaching for the phone even though it's not there, sensing phantom vibrations, or simply feeling "a little weird."

In Internet addiction, withdrawal can present as physical symptoms. Withdrawal can lead to cravings, and a craving goes beyond a desire to the point where your body actually physically thinks it needs the Internet. Some of the things that a person might experience when their use is limited include the following:

- Agitation
- Anger
- Anxiety
- Headache
- Light-headedness
- Rapid heartbeat
- Shortness of breath
- Tense muscles

The other side of the withdrawal coin in addiction is tolerance. This basically means that you need increasing amounts of a drug to get high. In the case of Internet addiction, you may need more and more time online to get a good feeling from the experience or you may need increasingly exciting online content or both.

PSYCHOSIS

As with any addiction, the problems that people experience from Internet addiction exist on a spectrum. Often people begin with very few side effects, but the more intense and prolonged the addiction, the worse those side effects are. People who get into extreme Internet addiction can experience heightened states of distress more commonly associated with drug addiction. For example, it is not unheard of for people to go into psychosis as a result of Internet addiction.

Psychosis is most likely to occur in Internet gaming addiction. Immersion in gaming, particularly highly realistic fantasy gaming for prolonged periods of time without rest, can lead to a break with reality so that the gamer ceases to know whether or not they're in the game. In psychological terms, the gamer may experience derealization (which is an inability to know what is real) and/or depersonalization (which is when the person doesn't feel real anymore). As mentioned previously, sleep deprivation can lead to HPA axis dysregulation, and one of the more serious symptoms of that is psychotic breakdown. This dysregulation is exacerbated by Internet use in a cycle.

Psychosis can occur during withdrawal from the Internet. For example, in 2012, two doctors reported on the case of a fifteen-year-old boy with Internet addiction whose parents removed the Internet. Within a few days, the boy had developed several psychotic symptoms including paranoia that his parents had stolen his passwords and were trying to learn secrets about him because they wanted to hurt him.

In that case, the child was treated with psychiatric medication. In other instances, removing devices and setting up a safe space during withdrawal have been shown to be enough to resolve psychosis. Because this is such an extreme reaction to Internet addiction, it hasn't been studied completely enough to know the best method of treatment. We will look further at treatment options in Chapter 7.

CHAPTER 3

What Makes the Internet So Addictive?

Addiction happens in the brain. It looks like it's happening on the outside, in the insertion of a needle into an arm, in the glazed-over eyes of the Internet addict who hasn't left the screen for thirty-six hours. However, the behavior is just the tip of the iceberg; the addiction is going on between the ears. Therefore, in order to understand what makes the Internet so addictive, we have to understand a little bit about the human brain.

Brain imaging studies have emerged in the past few decades, leading to an increasingly more in-depth understanding of the way that our brain works and of what addiction looks like in the brain. It is important to note, before delving into the research, though, that for all that we now know about the human brain, there is still so much to learn. The technology for brain study is new, plus Internet technology is new and changing, so we simply don't have the information that we need to be able to accurately say exactly what the long-term effects are on the brain with regard to daily use of Internet devices. That said, we do have a good idea about the initial effects and the relationship of Internet activity to behavioral addiction within the brain. We have early studies, and we are learning more and more each year.

One of the most powerful things that research has uncovered so far is that if you look at the brain scans of people addicted to technology, and you compare those with the brain scans of people addicted to drugs, you will be unable to tell a difference. The addiction looks the same in the brain regardless of the substance or behavior. This has led some neuroscientists and other professionals to use terms for the Internet such as "electronic heroin" or "electronic cocaine." This underlines the fact that despite contradictory arguments about whether or not Internet addiction is "real" or "problematic," brain research strongly shows that you can indeed get addicted to the Internet.

NEUROTRANSMITTERS: DOPAMINE AND THE REWARD SYSTEM

The brain is a complex thing, and it takes years of study to really get a grasp on how it works. So, we're only going to examine parts of it as they relate specifically to addiction. In doing so, we have to begin with the neurotransmitters. These are basically the communicators, or messengers, in the brain. They transmit information from one part to another, often from neuron to neuron. This information is critical to our survival; it tells the brain to perform certain important tasks such as eating and sleeping. Addictive behavior manipulates these neurotransmitters, causing disruption in the brain. You might not care so much about eating or sleeping because your brain isn't communicating the importance of that anymore. It's been hijacked by the drug. The drug could be the Internet.

Dopamine is perhaps the most important neurotransmitter at play when it comes to Internet addiction. It plays a really critical role in Internet usage in general and Internet addiction specifically. Dopamine is a natural drug in the brain, often called "the feel good chemical." Whenever we experience something that feels good, the brain releases dopamine. That dopamine goes directly to the nucleus accumbens, a cluster of nerve cells often called the "brain's pleasure center." These neurotransmitters communicate, "Ah, yes, that feels great." Here's basically what happens:

- Something makes you feel good.
- This sends a signal to the ventral tegmental area of the brain.
- That travels to the nucleus accumbens to tell you that you feel really, really good.
- Then your hippocampus records that feel-good experience as a memory.
- The amygdala creates a condition response that makes you want to do that again.

Dopamine itself is a bit addictive; we always want to feel good, so the more dopamine we get, the more we want to have. The brain is always seeking out things that will give it a dopamine release. The more dopamine we get from an activity, the more likely it is that the activity will become addictive. If you know that something feels good, you are going to keep going back to that same activity to try to get that food feeling.

One of the things that the brain especially loves is the feeling of novelty. Our brains are wired to take pleasure in new, unexpected things. When we experience something new, particularly something that feels especially good, our brains surge with dopamine. Therefore, we seek out novelty. The brain's reward center activates when we hit the jackpot by finding that novel thing. This relates to addiction generally in that people will constantly seek out new, better, more interesting triggers for that feel-good dopamine release. It relates specifically to Internet addiction because the Internet offers constant potential for something new. With just a quick click of the mouse, you can see something that you have never seen before. The Internet is designed to offer instant gratification, which is exactly what the brain loves—give me more of that dopamine, and give it to me now!

Research has found that intermittent rewards are much more satisfying to the brain than rewards delivered on a regular schedule. Think about it; if you know that every fifth bite of food will taste amazing, then your brain will habituate to that. You'll tune out to the first four bites and feel mildly excited by bite five. However, if you have no idea which bite of food is the one that will taste good, then you'll always be hopeful for it, and when that exciting flavor does hit your mouth, it will be that much more exciting. Now apply that to the Internet; you never really know whether the next web link, article, cat video, or social media post will be the one that excites your brain. That itself makes the search for something pleasurable even more enjoyable to the brain. That enjoyment is so addictive. Remember a few years back when the Shiba Inu Puppy Cam was all the rage? You could tune in day or night and peek in real time at what the growing puppies were doing. Often, they weren't doing anything. Sometimes they weren't even on the screen. But every now and then you'd tune in, and they'd be there acting super adorable and, you would feel great. You'd keep coming back.

We see intermittent rewards (also called a variable-ratio reward schedule) in online video games. Even a game as simple as *Minecraft*, which has a lower potential for addiction than real-time strategy games, offers the dopamine high of intermittent rewards. In the game, you attempt to find gold, but there is a moment right before your virtual pickaxe strikes down when you don't know whether or not the gold will be there. When it is, you feel great, and dopamine releases. If it's not there, you have that much stronger of an urge to try again. You were almost about to get that great dopamine surge, and then it didn't happen. Why would you stop now?!

Nicholas Kardaras calls that hit of dopamine a "brain orgasm." He has found through studies of brain imaging that Internet behaviors are as capable of stimulating the pleasure center as sexual activity is. This is potentially more dangerous than it seems at first glance. To understand, we have to look at evolution. Back in a time when we had to forage for our food, the brain released dopamine when we found and ate that food so that dopamine pleasure spike was really a key part of our survival. We wanted to feel good again, which motivated us to go out and look for more food. Therefore, natural dopamine is tied up with the circuits in the brain that relate to food, to sex, and essentially to survival.

Of course, most of us don't have to forage for our food today. We get instant gratification rewards all day long from various stimuli including the Internet. However, this confuses the body. Dopamine is naturally highest in the body when we seek food, sex, and safety. Therefore, when dopamine levels are high, the body thinks that is what is happening. The brain's reward system gets confused, actually beginning to believe that the behaviors (such as Internet searching or online gaming) are crucial to survival. The more frequently we indulge in the behavior, the longer those dopamine levels stay elevated and the more confused the body gets. The brain knows that it wants to feel good, and it knows that the addictive drug or behavior makes it feel that way. It thinks you will die without it.

This has the potential to increase addiction because cravings continue to intensify despite constantly elevated levels of dopamine. Moreover, it is possible that the dopamine we get from natural sources (like food and sex) can get dulled. We are so used to the dopamine high from technology that this "regular" dopamine doesn't feel good enough. Therefore, we seek more and more dopamine through technology in order to keep feeling good. It is as if we were going in there and tinkering with our brains, telling the brain that food and sex aren't that important to survival anymore, but the Internet is. Pause for a moment, and think about the consequences of that for the entire species, let alone the individual.

There are four different dopamine pathways in the brain, three of which relate to different aspects of reward. The mesocortical pathway is linked with cognitive and emotional abilities as well as memory, attention, and our ability to learn. The nigrostriatal pathway is all about movement and sensory stimulation. And the mesolimbic pathway is the pleasure-seeking and reward-desiring section. The latter is the one most associated with addiction. However, all of these areas may be affected by changes in dopamine levels.

If you're having trouble following this, Kevin Roberts gives a great analogy, describing the brain like a complicated highway system. He writes, "Addiction floods some roads with increased traffic, while allowing other roads to fall into disuse and disrepair." The pathways are different highways in this system, and the desire to get the reward is so strong that your brain will try different pathways to get there. The neurotransmitters, including dopamine, are the cars that you take to get from one place to another. You are on a highway to pleasure, and you're driving your car as fast and wildly as you can to get there.

Dopamine is only one of several important neurotransmitters in the brain. You have probably also heard of serotonin. People with depression often have chemical imbalances particularly in terms of the serotonin levels. Serotonin is your brain's biggest mood stabilizer. It also plays a role in your systems for sleep, food, and sexual desire.

Much of the research into the neurochemistry of addiction has focused on dopamine, so we currently have less understanding about the way that addiction relates to serotonin and some of the other transmitters. One thing we do know for sure is that the nucleus accumbens (that pleasure center in the brain) consists of two of the major neurotransmitters: dopamine and serotonin. Therefore, we can guess that when addiction messes with that reward center in the brain, it includes serotonin effects. We also know that serotonin is directly linked to our mood, so some of the consequences of Internet addiction discussed in the previous chapter (depression, irritability, etc.) may be linked with serotonin changes in the brain caused by the additive behavior.

Here's something else that's interesting: if serotonin is low, then the effects of dopamine motivation are greater. In other words, if you have low serotonin, then you're more likely to seek out the things that give you a feel-good hit of dopamine. This makes sense; low serotonin means feeling depressed or low in mood, and you don't want to feel that way, so your brain makes up for it by seeking out that dopamine hit. The reason this is important is because whether or not the Internet affects serotonin levels, we do know from early research that people who start out with low serotonin are more at risk of developing Internet addiction. They're more motivated than others to seek the dopamine hit that the Internet may provide.

One study published in the 2011 issue of *Neuropsychopharmacology* explored the role of serotonin in gambling addiction, which we know is a behavioral addiction similar to Internet addiction. The study looked specifically at "loss chasing," which refers to the gambler's addicted behavior to try to cover their losses by gambling even more. They found that there was a relationship between serotonin and the willingness to loss chase, noting specifically that serotonin plays a complex, little-understood role, in impulse control not the least of which is that it plays a part in mediating how we learn about negative events. So, if serotonin is off, then we don't make the best choices about things that are affecting us negatively. Combine that with seeking the dopamine hit, and the whole system is primed for addiction.

Another neurotransmitter that's been linked with potential Internet addiction harm is gamma-aminobutyric acid (GABA). Among other things, GABA communicates to help control vision and motor function. More important, it plays a crucial role in inhibiting neuron activity in order to reduce stress and increase relaxation, which in turn can lead to a more balanced mood, better sleep, and even pain relief. In order to feel "right," you need to have the right GABA activity. Research indicates that Internet use messes with that.

A small study presented by Hyung Suk Seo, MD, professor of neuroradiology at Korea University, found that people diagnosed with Internet addiction had more GABA activity than those without addiction. This further means that GABA levels were off in terms of the ratio to other activity in the brain. Increased GABA can lead to problems with both cognitive and emotional processing, as well as to addiction side effects such as fatigue and anxiety.

Finally, let's talk about norepinephrine. This neurotransmitter plays a role that's similar to adrenaline, activating the body's "fight, flight, or freeze" response. When your body thinks that it's in danger, you experience changes in heart rate, breathing, body temperature, and your ability to process sensory stimuli. This can affect your movement (thus, you fight or flee or sometimes freeze). It can also affect your mood, sleep, appetite, and so forth. Basically, your body goes into a state of focusing entirely on getting to safety, so it doesn't care as much about those other things.

There's an interesting history when it comes to the research around norepinephrine and addiction. Back in the 1960s and 1970s, researchers were sure that it played a key role in addiction. However, those early experiments were limited, and researchers couldn't quite tell whether it was norepinephrine or dopamine at play. By the 1980s, almost all of the research began to focus on dopamine. That is why we have so much information today about the role that dopamine plays in addiction but much less information about the role of the other neurotransmitters including norepinephrine.

More recent studies are beginning to try to fill in this gap, and they do indicate that norepinephrine is worth studying if we want to know more about addiction. They're also shedding more light on the original confusing studies between norepinephrine and dopamine. The truth is, although we are learning more and more about the roles of each individual neurotransmitter, the brain exists as a thing in its entirety. It's not just the individual parts that matter but also the way that those parts interact with one another. Some of the dopamine pathways, including the mesolimbic pathway, are modulated in part by norepinephrine. If one part gets affected, then so do the other parts. So, although we don't have all of the answers, we do know that addiction happens in the brain, and within the brain it happens in large part among the communication systems of which the neurotransmitters play the biggest role. And studies indicate that the Internet is messing with the brain. To what degree and whether this is good, bad, or neutral is up for debate, and perhaps only time will tell.

THE FRONTAL LOBE AND PREFRONTAL CORTEX

If you look at physical models of the brain, then you will see that it contains four paired lobes (one in the right hemisphere and one in the left): occipital, temporal, parietal, and frontal. Each lobe is responsible for certain body functions. For example, the occipital lobe relates to vision. The frontal lobe is responsible for voluntary movement and cognitive functions. This is the part of the brain that helps us with "higher-level" functioning such as problem-solving, planning, and regulating our emotions. Our memories and personality are formed here. It also plays a part in the actions we choose, such as running, and in managing attention including selective attention abilities (what to pay attention to and what to ignore).

The frontal lobe, as the name suggests, is located at the front of the brain. And right at the front of the frontal lobe is the prefrontal cortex. The human brain develops back to front, so this is the last part of the brain to fully develop. And it's the most complex part of the human brain in terms of allowing us adults to do the things that other mammals—or even children—can't quite grasp. Attention, planning, prioritizing, impulse control behavior, emotional control, and adjusting to complicated and varying situations are all things that we are able to do thanks to the prefrontal cortex.

Brain injuries often affect the prefrontal cortex. They can change a person's ability to perform executive functions, so someone who could normally plan things very well and stay organized can't do so anymore after a traumatic brain injury. They may get emotionally dysregulated, have trouble controlling themselves, and even experience complete personality changes. Clearly, this is an important part of the brain.

Like so much else when it comes to Internet addiction, it's hard to tell cause and effect here. Research indicates that people who have problems in their prefrontal cortex are more likely to be at risk for Internet addiction.

Other research has found that regular, ongoing addictive behavior has a negative impact on the brain, inhibiting the abilities of the prefrontal cortex. This part of the brain may literally shrink with addictive Internet use. Since this is the part of the brain that regulates impulse control, the more damaged it gets, the less able we are to make logical, long-term solutions. In other words, addiction begets more addictive behavior; you can't choose the actions that end addiction when your brain is wired to respond to impulsive drives that get triggered in addiction.

Did you catch what we said there just a few sentences ago? It bears repeating: this part of the brain may literally shrink with addictive Internet use. Multiple studies have found that the brain actually shrinks, possibly as much as 20 percent, losing more and more area with longer duration of the addiction. We lose parts of our brain when we engage in addictive Internet behavior. The frontal lobe decreases in size. Studies have also found brain shrinkage in the striatum and the insula, areas related to appropriate social behavior and developing empathy and compassion. People with Internet addiction are literally losing their minds in ways that affect their ability to participate healthily in our society. Notably, the studies into this are young, and there's some debate about them within the scientific community. However, enough information has been released that a large percentage of reputable researchers believe that Internet addiction can lead to brain shrinkage.

GRAY MATTER AND WHITE MATTER

When we talk about parts of the brain like the prefrontal cortex, we're talking about gray matter. When we talk about the brain shrinking due to Internet addiction, it's the gray matter that shrinks. But the brain consists of both gray matter and white matter, and both may be affected by Internet addiction. The gray matter is the bulk of what we see when we look at a human brain—the wrinkled, pinkish-gray tissue consisting of cell bodies, dendrites, and nerve synapses. But these gray matter tissues are connected by bundles of axons called white matter. White matter exists in the brain and the spinal cord; although there's some gray matter in the spinal cord, it's mostly white matter there.

One important thing to know about when it comes to white matter is the role of myelin, an insulating layer that wraps around the white matter. It's a protective part of the body. Among other functions, it helps to make those axons more efficient, allowing brains to do more and to do so more quickly.

As the brain develops, learning experiences are solidified with myelin. For example, when a child first learns to read, the areas of the brain that are used in reading get increased myelin, and (barring some tragic brain event) the child will then forever know how to read. Myelination is what we're talking about when we talk about something being "hardwired in the brain." It's an amazing process, and it doesn't stop when we hit puberty; a healthy brain can continue growing and myelinating for about five decades. With myelin, we learn; without it, we are vulnerable to a series of problems including an inability to focus, pay attention, feel empathy, and even discern reality.

But there are many different things in our environment that reduce the healthiness of the brain and impact its ability to keep growing white matter. A range of things—from toxins to stress—can cause problems with this part of our brains, limiting our ability to hardwire learning. One of the things that can cause such problems is overstimulation. Think about how overstimulating the Internet is. Naturally, it's going to affect our white matter. This is a particular issue for younger brains that go through key developmental periods in which myelin-strengthening is not only at its peak but also at its most vulnerable.

China-based research indicates a direct link between Internet addiction and myelin. People diagnosed with Internet addiction disorder in one study had problems with myelin in the areas of the brain that are related to decision-making, emotional generation, executive attention, and the ability to store and retrieve information. The white matter carries information from one part of the brain to the other so that the whole brain can operate properly. When it's depleted, the connections don't work as well. For example, your brain doesn't properly connect the lower emotional impulses and the higher cognitive management, so you might not be as capable of thinking before you act.

This research supports what other brain studies have found about addiction in general. It changes the brain.

NEUROPLASTICITY

You have probably heard about neuroplasticity before. Also called brain plasticity or neuroelasticity, it refers to the brain's ability to change and grow over time. It's truly an amazing thing. When someone experiences a brain injury, they may be unable to do certain things because that part of the brain is hindered, but through therapy they can create new neural pathways that allow them to resume function. The brain can learn again.

There are two types of neuroplasticity: synaptic and cellular. Synaptic neuroplasticity is a change in the strength of the connection across the junction from one brain cell to the next (synapse). Cellular neuroplasticity is a change in the number of brain cells that are talking to one another. Synaptic neuroplasticity is lifelong (an old dog can learn new tricks), but cellular neuroplasticity primarily happens early in life. About 90 percent of our cellular structure is set by the age of six and the rest through to age twenty-five.

In fact, we get an overabundance of brain cells when we're babies. We grow really fast. We can learn much faster as children than we can as adults. We get a lot of brain cells really fast, and then the cells go through a pruning process; what you don't use you lose, and what you do use grows and strengthens. Therefore, it's especially important to pay attention to what we are and aren't feeding into our brains while the brain is still in that pruning process. That said, because of neuroplasticity, habitual behaviors can change the brain at any point in time.

Neuroplasticity means that if we do something regularly, it will change the brain. It may change some of the cells. It will certainly change the synaptic connections. The behavior we engage in every day shapes the brain. Now think about some of our common online behavior, things that we have all gotten just a little bit too comfortable with since the Internet became so prevalent in our worlds. Let your mind wander for a moment to all of the things you did or saw online in the past week: social media posts you scrolled past in less than one second, comments you read in a few seconds or wrote in under a minute, memes that quickly made you laugh before you rapidly forwarded them to someone else, stories you browsed while multitasking, and . . . the list goes on. All of those are very short, addictive behaviors that are teaching our neural pathways to skim, stay shallow, see information and pass it along but not retain it, and quickly jump from thought to thought.

If that's what we're teaching our neural pathways, at what expense are we doing so? Remember, the habits we do every day create those pathways. When we stop doing them, the pathways start to fade. We're teaching our brain those quick-fix activities at the expense of deep thought, focused attention, and memory retention.

This is your brain on the Internet.

Your Brain Is Susceptible and Businesspeople Know It

As you can see, your brain is designed in such a manner that it is super-sensitive to the potential for addiction. Some people are more at risk than others due to their own natural brain chemistry and brain structure. Someone with damage to their prefrontal cortex or with naturally low serotonin levels may be at more risk of addiction than someone without those things. But all brains are at risk. And the people who are selling us this technology are well aware of that risk. In fact, they are in the business of exploiting it.

The companies that develop the devices, the apps, the websites, and the advertising all benefit when you spend more time on those things. They want you to become addicted. In fact, there are countless stories of some of the biggest names in technology making sure to limit their own children's exposure to technology precisely because they're so aware of how addictive it is designed to be.

Several industry insiders have pointed out the similarity of apps and devices to slot machines. It's no casual comment. Some of the designers behind these tools have specifically studied the psychology of slot machines and then adapted their techniques to computers and smartphones. They prey upon the brain's desire for intermittent reward by creating tools that provide exactly that. They do it so that they can make money. When they show up to the table to ask for more venture capital, they have to show that more and more people are using their product, that they're using it for longer, and that they keep coming back to use it more and more. So, if you find yourself checking a particular app or site more often over time, staying on it longer, and talking to others who are doing the same, it's likely because it was designed that way. In fact, there are people who have full-time jobs specifically to aid in addictive design; although some companies use creative names that hide that this is what they're doing, more and more are offering job positions for "demand engineers" or "attention engineering" positions. People get paid, often mightily so, to demand your attention.

Technology author Nir Eyal spent several years studying how different companies were getting people addicted and distilled it down to a four-step process he calls the hooked model. Through this model, companies are able to repeatedly get customers back again and again without expensive or aggressive advertising, and they do so by manipulating people's existing habits. The four steps are as follows:

1. The trigger, which may be external or internal. For example, you get an external trigger when your phone notifies you that you have a new message on an app that you just downloaded. Each time you get a notification, it triggers you to check the app. You feel good when you get a good experience on the app, so you start to associate the app with good feelings. Then whenever you feel bad, which is an internal trigger, you turn to the app to feel better. It hooks you with both external and internal triggers.

2. The action, which is the thing that you do (eventually out of habit) in an effort to get the reward that you associate with the trigger. You open the app, you click the link, you hit the like, and you enter the giveaway.
3. The intermittent reward, which Eyal calls the variable reward. This is the part where you may or may not get that dopamine hit. You're eagerly anticipating it. Technology and media companies exploit this part of the model more than anything else. They have studied that your brain doesn't like predictable rewards, but rather it likes intermittent ones, and they have designed their products accordingly. In fact, you'll find that you often get more rewards in the beginning than later because once your brain is addicted, you don't need as many rewards. So, for example, a game might offer you lots of bonuses and coins in the early levels and fewer as you get to higher levels.
4. The investment, which is what you've given to the tool that makes you even more likely to get and stay addicted to it. Why do you think so many of today's products give you a bonus to share with your friends? It's not just because the company will get one more follower that way. It's because when you share, you've invested, and therefore, you yourself are more likely to grow your own addiction. Depending on the product or tool, you might invest time, energy, money, social capital, or data. For example, investing the time to learn the new features on a favorite app makes you even more likely to keep using that app.

This is just one model of how the addictive nature of technology works, but it points to the fact that companies are all aware of your brain's addictive nature. They want to take advantage of it because they benefit when you become addicted. In a well-known 2017 episode of Bill Maher's *Real Time*, cited in Cal Newport's book *Digital Minimalism*, Maher directly compares "the tycoons of social media" to tobacco farmers. Historically, Big Tobacco exploited addiction, particularly in children, to sell their products, and Maher, among others, argues that social media giants (and other leaders in technology and media) are doing exactly the same thing. They know it's addictive, they know it's changing our brains and affecting our health and relationships, and they are exploiting it anyway because they want to sell their product.

Consider, for example, how we have already gotten so used to predictive text and targeted advertising. When you go to type something into

Google, it fills in possible responses for you. Whenever you are online, you see ads that are targeted just to you. These things can prey upon your existing addictive tendencies. For example, if you search for a dating app, you'll suddenly start seeing all sorts of ads for dating or about being single. This can lead you to follow more and more links and download more and more similar apps. Companies do this on purpose.

CHAPTER 4

Internet Addiction and Relationships

We have already looked at how Internet addiction can affect relationships. Now it's time to look at different types of Internet addiction, and it is interesting to learn that many of these addictions are themselves related to online relationships.

There are two broad types of Internet addiction: general and specific. People with general Internet addiction are simply addicted to the act of spending time on their devices, without too much focus on any specific content. Most people, though, have a specific addiction, which means that they are only addicted to very specific content.

A lot of content online involves or simulates human relationships, so it's of very little surprise that a lot of specific addictions relate to that content. This also makes sense with human psychology and culture. We are social creatures. Our entire being is primed to exist in relationship with others. We seek approval from others, we want to fit in with them, and we often define ourselves in relation to others. For better or worse (and in the case of addiction, it's often for worse), we increasingly utilize technology to facilitate, enhance, or even simulate our need for social connection and inclusivity. All of the specific addictions in this chapter relate to relationships and include addictions to social media, texting, and compulsive use of dating apps. Pornography addiction, which is one of the most widely studied forms of Internet addiction, also falls into this category.

SOCIAL MEDIA ADDICTION

One of the most common types of Internet addiction is addiction to the use of social media. This is due in part to the content itself; the relationships online are compelling enough to garner our attention. However, the design of the sites is what really makes them addictive, and social media designers have been tweaking that design steadily to increase addictive qualities. The sites want people coming back frequently, and they create incentives to do so, which can lead to or exacerbate addictive use.

Social media launched back in the late 1990s, but it didn't become widely used until the convergence of broadband Internet and smartphones. More and more people were getting online, and they were doing it more often since the Internet was now at their fingertips, and this opened the door to truly connecting those people. Facebook launched in 2004; Instagram launched in 2010.

Back in the early days of social media, including the beginning of Facebook, the purpose—and the reason that people spent time on the device—was to connect with other people that they already knew in real life. People spent time on the site as a novelty, because it was fun and somewhat social, but it didn't dominate their attention. Over the years, Facebook has added countless tools designed to exploit the brain's addictive nature.

Take, for example, the "like" button. Do you remember back in the early days when it wasn't there at all? The button actually wasn't introduced until 2009, five years after the company launched. Why did Facebook add that button? Author and social psychologist Adam Alter posits that it marks the turning point in how Facebook has changed to become more addictive, because it shifted the platform from one in which you passively perused updates to one in which you were an interactive participant. This exploits several of those addictive features that the human brain loves including the following:

- Once you've hit the like button, you're more invested in the interaction. Therefore, you're more likely to come back to the site, spend more time there, and share it more with others.
- You never know when you post whether people are going to hit the like for you or not. This satisfies the brain's love for intermittent rewards. The more you post, the more likely it is that you'll get some likes, so you start posting more and checking more frequently on your likes status.
- Humans want social approval. The like tells us, at least in theory, that people approve of us. That feels good, so we want to keep doing it.

At least two of the people on the original team that designed the Facebook like button (project manager Leah Pearlman and engineer Justin Rosenstein) have come out publicly to explain how addictive it is and that it was designed to be so. So, make no mistake, of all of the content out there on the Internet today, social media is among the most addictive, in large part because businesses have spent a lot of time, money, and energy to make it so.

But what exactly is a social media addiction? Essentially, it means that you keep using social media with increasing frequency even though the rewards that you get from it are diminishing and/or there are negative consequences in other areas of your life. For example, if you find yourself spending time connecting with people on social media at the expense of your face-to-face relationships, that can be a sign of an addiction. You aren't getting as much from that online interaction as you could from face-to-face connection, plus your real-life connections begin to suffer, and yet you can't stop yourself.

Of course, it's challenging to tell when use has become abuse. In trying to determine whether someone has a social media addiction, it's common to use a question-based assessment. One example comes from psychologists Mark Griffiths and Daria Kuss, who work out of Nottingham Trent University to study the impact of technology on behavior. They offer the following six questions for basic assessment:

1. When you are not online, do you think about using social media?
2. Do you experience increasing urges to use social media over time?
3. Is social media a way that you try to forget about your problems?
4. Do you continue to use social media even after you've decided you want to stop?
5. Do you become restless or upset when you are unable to use social media?
6. Has there been a negative impact on your relationships, work, or school because of your use of social media?

People who answer yes to a majority of those questions might have an addiction to social media. Moreover, if you're experiencing consequences and have withdrawal and tolerance to social media use, then there's probably a problem.

In a 2017 paper written by Griffiths and Kuss, the authors lay out some important conclusions about social media and its potential for addiction. They emphasize that you can utilize social media without becoming addicted to it, but that social networking is a way of being that you can easily become addicted to. They note that within social media addiction, there are specific addictions that include Facebook addiction as well as specific disordered thoughts and behavior including nomophobia (fear of being without a smartphone) and FOMO (fear of missing out).

In this paper, the authors also lay out some helpful models for defining social media addiction:

- *Biopsychosocial model.* This is built upon our understanding of addictive substances and extends to addictive behaviors. Addiction is viewed in terms of mood changes, preoccupation with use, problems in other areas of life resulting from addiction, and withdrawal, tolerance, and relapse.
- *Cognitive behavioral model.* A person has maladaptive beliefs that are "exacerbated through a number of external issues," and this leads to social media addiction.
- *Social skills model.* A person has difficulty with face-to-face social interaction and turns to social media as a substitute, leading to addiction.
- *Socio-cognitive model.* A person has a good experience with social media, then expects to continue to have that experience, and begins to use the sites excessively in search of that despite not always getting what they want out of it.

These are different lenses for looking at social media addiction (and Internet addiction more generally) that lead us back to the brain and the psychology of humans. People who are interested in working professionally with Internet addicts, such as counselors, can utilize these different models for helping to both assess and understand a person's addiction to social media. Through psychoeducation, they can help their clients better understand the issue as well.

As mentioned, an individual may have a general social media addiction, or they may have a very specific addiction to one aspect of social media use. This can be an addiction to only one specific platform. For example, someone may be able to take or leave Instagram but have an addiction to Twitter. Another person may have a Facebook addiction but not use any other social media at all. The specific platform isn't the only thing that people can become addicted to though; it's also possible to develop an addiction for certain activities on one or more sites.

For example, you can become addicted to the act of taking and posting selfies or to the act of catfishing others.

Selfies

Selfie addiction sounds a little bit ridiculous if you've never encountered someone who struggles with this problem. However, it's quite a serious issue for a small group of people. Some people will take hundreds of photos of one pose just to make sure that they have the best one to post on social media. After posting, they look obsessively at the comments people are making, and their mood and self-esteem can be greatly impacted by what they see there. They'll delete a photo within minutes if it hasn't gotten the quick, positive reception that they expected, and they can feel terrible about themselves for hours afterward as a result.

Instead of, or in addition to, taking many photos, a person with a selfie addiction might spend hours tweaking one photo just to get it right. They'll use different apps and filters to perfect the lighting, erase their perceived flaws, and enhance certain traits in order to appear exactly as they want to appear. It becomes an obsession, and this obsession leads to addiction. They keep taking and tweaking more and more photos, looking for the perfect one, never quite satisfied. Every once in a while, they'll get the image or response to an image that feels great, and it'll offer that big hit of dopamine, and then the cycle starts again.

Selfie addiction is often inextricably linked with self-image issues. When you're constantly trying to tweak your appearance for the perfect photo, it's hard to be satisfied with the way you look in real life. As you zoom in on the screen, you see all of your (real or perceived) flaws magnified. This can lead to, or exist in combination with, body dysmorphic disorder, a mental health condition in which the person obsesses over their flaws, grooms and exercises excessively, avoids mirrors, constantly works to change their appearance, and obviously has negative self-esteem. Whether or not a selfie addiction gets to that extreme, someone with this addiction is at risk of basing too much of their self-worth on their image to the point that it causes problems with both physical and mental health.

As we've seen, a characteristic of addiction is that it causes problems in a key area of your life. In the case of selfie addiction, the person might spend so much time trying to get their images to look a certain way that they don't actually do the things they desire to do. In extreme cases, the individual might live an entirely fake life. For example, they might invest in thousands of dollars of props to make it look like they're at the beach in their photos. Meanwhile, they're really never leaving the house. They're spending so much time and energy on that online image that they can't even afford a beach vacation.

That's an extreme example, of course. In most cases, the person will actually attend the events in the photos. However, they may not be enjoying them or participating fully, because they are obsessed with getting the right photos to post later. Let's say that a man focuses so much on his appearance and the right photos at a mixer that he fails to do the networking that would land him a job that he really wants. This is an example of someone whose real life is negatively impacted by his selfie addiction.

Selfie addiction can also negatively impact real-life relationships. There is a 2018 Taco Bell commercial that captures this perfectly. Most commonly known as "Sunset Heart Hands," it features an "Instagram boyfriend" whose primary role in his relationship seems to be to take cute photos of his girlfriend to post on Instagram. Then he discovers a new Taco Bell item, so his hands are full, and he can't take the photos. She starts insistently repeating the phrase, "Sunset Heart Hands," because she desperately wants him to take the all-so-often-posted image of her fingers forming a heart that frames the sunset. She gets increasingly agitated; he says, "Let's just enjoy the moment," and she snaps. Of course, this is an ad for Taco Bell and it's not exactly a selfie, but it dramatizes an increasingly common problem—the couple selfie that becomes more important than just being together in the moment. The addict becomes so obsessed with documenting their relationship together online that the actual relationship suffers. This brings us directly into a different, but related (and often intertwined), social media addiction: an addiction to curating the "perfect" life.

The Self-Curated "Perfect" Life

This type of addiction goes beyond the selfie to include an addiction to posting pictures of your room or home, pets, clothing, children and family, vacations, and so forth. In addiction you don't merely want to record and share some your favorite things from your life; you want to make everything look perfect in your online world. This can impact your real life. For example, are you ignoring that your dog is completely stressed out by the outfit you've put him in and the camera always in his face? Or have you failed to notice that your child never actually gets to enjoy the experience of feeding the ducks because you're so consumed with getting her to pose properly for the duck-feeding picture? As with "Sunset Heart Hands," these small things add up day after day to eat away at your relationships and diminish the quality of your actual life experience.

As with selfie addiction, the addiction can be to taking multiple photos, tweaking photos, and/or seeing the response that those photos receive on your social media platforms. The addict may pay constant attention to the number of followers they have from day to day, feeling devastated when they lose some and elated when they gain a few. They may get a huge surge of dopamine when one of their images gets reposted by a bigger account, validating the idea that their life is "perfect." However, the addict often feels like a fraud, because they know that there's a mess cropped out of the image and that nothing is perfect at all. This can lead to a cycle of trying to perfect the next image even more to try to escape being "found out."

This belief that you're a fraud is a condition often called imposter syndrome. And this can lead you to feel depressed about your own life while simultaneously making you feel like you have to keep up with this perfect online charade. This experience also exacerbates any pain that you already experience about unrealized dreams you may have; it looks like everyone else is living the life that you want to have. You don't want to feel that pain, so you desire an escape, and social media offers the perfect, terrible escape so you become more and more addicted.

Internet marketer Morra Aarons-Mele writes about this in her book *Hiding in the Bathroom: An Introvert's Roadmap to Getting Out There (When You'd Rather Stay Home)* when she criticizes what she calls "achievement porn." She talks about how achievement has been fetishized thanks in large part to social media images of the peak experiences of life. For example, a pregnant mother might feel like she has to contort herself into the perfect glowing yoga pose on a cliff side in her second trimester to get the perfect image of her "perfect pregnancy." So, even something as natural as pregnancy becomes a subject for achievement in photos. The person suffering from an addiction to this is constantly performing for the camera, seeking validation through images. She may eventually start to feel like she doesn't even know what's true about herself anymore. This sense of being out of touch with your inner self can wreak havoc on your mental health.

Relative to this, someone addicted to curating the perfect online life often grapples with the feeling that they don't measure up to the other people that they see online. Human beings have a natural tendency to compare ourselves to others. To the addict, it may always look like someone else's house is better decorated, their closet filled with cuter purchases, their food prepared more perfectly, and their friends happier in photos. If you suffer from this, then you keep trying to make your life look that same way, but you never quite feel like you measure up. You can become increasingly dissatisfied with your own (normal) life because it doesn't match what you see in pictures. And yet, you can't seem to stop yourself from looking. You have to know what other people's pictures look like. You may become particularly obsessed with specific influencers or feeds, feeling jealous of them as you strive to match their following. This leads us to another type of social media addiction: stalking others.

Addiction to Other People's Content

Social media has stoked the human drive toward voyeurism. Although frequently associated with sexuality, voyeurism more generally means that you take pleasure in watching someone else, particularly when they're doing something private, dangerous, or scandalous. Social media has put everyone's private lives out there for all of us to see. Watching what someone is eating for dinner has become a very regular part of our everyday lives, and that is one of the more mundane things we get to glimpse each day. Some people share every waking moment of their lives on social media, and other people can get addicted to following those lives online.

An addiction to someone else's content can develop into stalking behavior. Stalking encompasses a broad spectrum of things that range from quietly obsessing over the person and following them online without contacting them to full-blown, in-real-life following them and causing them fear if not actual harm. Of course, most people with an addiction to other people's content don't become dangerous real-life stalkers, but given the right (or rather wrong) brain chemistry and environmental factors, it can happen. Alternatively, someone with unhealthy stalking tendencies can now easily find and follow their object of desire online and become addicted to tracking them in that way.

This type of social media addiction may manifest as becoming an online "superfan" of one or more people, usually celebrities or online influencers. The addict begins to feel like they are part of the person's life because they see everything that the other person is doing. They think that they truly know the person. And they may come to think that they have a relationship with that person, feeling hurt or offended when the person doesn't post in a timely manner, respond to a comment, or follow back the addict's account. The superfan may comment on every single post, tag the object of their addiction in all of their own images, and follow link after link after link to try to learn more about the person's life. They may contact the person through direct messaging, and if that fails, try to connect with the person's other online friends and followers.

As mentioned, all of the addictions discussed in this chapter relate to people's relationships, and that is particularly true with this type of social media addiction. Another way that it can manifest is through online addiction to the content of someone you know in real life. The most prevalent example is in the case of breakups; the relationship ends, but one or both partners become addicted to stalking the other on social media as a way to maintain something of the relationship. Other types of addiction, besides to an ex's content, could be to the content of their new partner or to the content of someone they have a crush on and want to get involved with.

It's one thing to Google a potential new partner to learn some basic things about them; it's another entirely to fall down the rabbit hole of reading every old post they ever made on social media and trying to analyze it for clues about where your own relationship might go.

Yet another way that this form of addiction can show up is when you become addicted to checking your partner's accounts. Jealousy as it relates to social media is a significant problem in many modern relationships. The more you look at your partner's online activity, the more your mind whirls and the more you try to soothe it with even more information, blowing it up into a full-blown addiction by stalking their social media accounts.

Fear of Missing Out

Many of the people who develop a social media addiction, particularly an addiction to other people's content, are driven by a fear of missing out (FOMO). This is the feeling that other people are online doing something interesting and that if you fail to get online as well, then you're going to be excluded from the fun. The term was originally coined by MTV who had found that even though 66 percent of young people found it exhausting to constantly be online, 58 percent worried that they were missing out on something if they didn't check in.

FOMO itself predicts addictive use; the more prone you are to the feeling, the more likely you'll engage in addictive behavior. It's a cyclical problem; more use leads to greater FOMO. FOMO has been associated with lower feelings of life satisfaction, well-being, and general mood and with increased likelihood of engaging in risky online behavior. FOMO can affect anyone, but it's particularly a problem for young users, who are in a stage of life when acceptance and inclusion with peers is at a high point.

People who are driven to use social media out of FOMO are more likely than others to develop addictive behavior. Author Larry Rosen explains that there are two major reasons people will compulsively use technology; FOMO being one of them. The other reason would be that they really love the experience. People who are driven by pleasure may still develop addictive behavior, but the pain of not using the device is worse for people who are driven by fear (or FOMO).

Author Morra Aarons-Mele emphasizes that FOMO can be a particular problem for people with introverted personalities. The introvert doesn't necessarily want to be out there in the world doing the things that people are sharing on social media. However, they may feel like they should be, like they are missing out on opportunities for growth, because of those introvert tendencies. Social media is a way to check in and feel connected to experiences without having to get out there.

In fact, social media relies on FOMO as a marketing strategy. The creators of social media want you to fear that you are missing out so that you'll keep checking back in to the app. The more time you spend there, the more money they make. Therefore, they exploit your fear to keep you active on the site. Coming back again and again becomes an addiction.

It is important to note that FOMO affects people of all ages. The quirky MTV-coined term often makes people think it only applies to teens. It can also make it seem like it's a problem that isn't that big of a deal. However, it can impact people's lives in deep and lasting ways. In her book *I Can't Help Myself*, advice columnist and author Meredith Goldstein wrote about how FOMO has affected the lives of the people she knows who are in their twenties and thirties. She shares that these people are overwhelmingly miserable in their day-to-day lives. They often feel like the slightest thing is the end of the world. She attributes this catastrophizing to FOMO. She explains that the plethora of opportunities available makes them feel that every single decision could be the wrong one. It relates to FOMO because, thanks to social media, they "know the specifics of every lost opportunity." For example, after a decision to move to New York instead of Los Angeles, a person might enviously see all of the beautiful lives being lived out in Los Angeles and mistakenly feel like they made the wrong choice. There is a constant reminder of the road not taken, and it can make the FOMO-motivated addict feel like all of their choices were the wrong ones.

Catfishing

Catfishing is the act of pretending to be someone else online in order to lure one or more people into a relationship with your fake persona. Catfishing can become addictive behavior for the person doing the catfishing, and it can naturally be intertwined with the addiction to curating a perfect life. A catfish can also exploit the social media addiction of others to secure victims.

A person addicted to catfishing might spend hours each day honing their fake profile. These days, most people can tell if a social media page or website looks a little bit fishy. If you want to really trick someone, you have to make it look good. On Facebook, for example, this means that you flesh out the page with photos taken at different places. The catfish steals someone else's photos, so they spend time searching online for suitable images and then tweaking them to add them to their profiles.

The catfish will not only fill out the profile. They have to make the interaction on the page look real. They add a variety of friends, communicating with these people regularly to generate comments on the page. In some cases, the catfish crafts full fake profiles of people to friend the original page to make it look even more realistic. The MTV reality television show *Catfish* has countless examples of people doing this.

This is all in addition to the time spent actually doing the catfishing. That's time spent finding people to catfish, searching the profile for information to prey upon, chatting and sharing messages and photos, and further developing the relationship. People catfish for a number of reasons including the following:

- *Low self-esteem.* They want to make friends online but don't feel like the people they want to know would like them the way that they really are.
- *Desire to connect with someone they know in real life.* For example, they want a romantic relationship with their best friend but are afraid to say so, so they make a fake profile to start the relationship as someone else.
- *Reconnecting with someone they know but aren't in touch with anymore.* For example, creating a fake profile to continue talking with an ex.
- *Conning people out of money.* Some catfishers are con artists who get money or other material goods from the people whom they catfish.

Any of these reasons for becoming a catfish in the first place can become addictive. You can become addicted to being the fake person that you've created. You can become addicted to the relationships you've created. You can become addicted to the "high" of getting away with it.

Why would someone fall prey to a catfish? Sometimes, it's as simple as really believing the best in people and assuming that everyone is who they say they are. However, it's often driven by something else. Loneliness, periods of grief and self-doubt, and low self-esteem of the victim are all possible reasons that someone would be susceptible to catfishing. Another key reason is that the victim already has a social media addiction. They spend so much time online already that they don't sense the warning signs of a stranger interacting with them there.

The way that the catfish interacts with the person can also worsen the victim's social media addiction. The catfish feeds the victim positive thoughts and feelings of validation, so of course the victim wants to hop online frequently to find out if they have a message that will give them that dopamine high.

Cyberbullying/Trolling

Just like someone can become addicted to the act of catfishing, it's possible to become addicted to other negative online behaviors including cyberbullying and trolling. Cyberbullying is persistent bullying of one or more people that takes place through apps, text, and social media. Trolling is when someone purposely posts inflammatory comments online in order to get a group riled up and engaging negatively. Both have similar roots and can become addictive for similar reasons.

People bully or troll others in large part because it gives them feelings of power and control. People who engage in these behaviors often have low self-esteem, symptoms of anxiety and/or depression, or problems at home or are in some way discontent with themselves and their lives. Instead of resolving those issues, they make themselves feel bigger and better by diminishing others. Although this can play out in real life, it's much easier to bully or troll people online than it is in person. You can do it anonymously, without many real-life consequences, and still derive the faux pleasure of feeling like you've done something powerful. If you've made someone cry because of your bullying online, then you've caused a reaction, which can give you a sense of control. Likewise, if you are able to generate a huge online fight about a topic through trolling, you've essentially controlled an entire crowd of people.

That feeling of power becomes addictive. The addict wants more of it to keep feeling powerful and in control. The Internet moves fast, and people's attention doesn't stick for long. In order to keep feeling powerful, the addict has to increase the frequency and intensity of their actions.

In a comprehensive Vice Motherboard article about whether or not trolling is addictive, writer Virginia Pelley describes a troller pseudonymed Dave who argued obsessively with people online under both his real name and several fake names, increasingly ruining his relationships with people in real life and even threatening his job security. For him, what was addictive was that he got to feel like he was right about things as he laid his arguments out for the world to see. He stopped caring about the real effects his arguments were having on people, including his own sister and childhood friends, because he was addicted to trolling.

George Caspar is a former Internet troll who shares his story in an e-book that describes how all of his troll behavior was motivated by shame. In a blog post about the book, he says that he has a shame-based personality, which is also an addictive personality, because in an effort not to feel shame, he tries to escape through behavior that becomes addictive. He highlights that the troll (and one could argue also the cyberbully) often particularly loves to shame their targets, and the reason is because they themselves feel so much shame. This doesn't justify the behavior but can explain some of the motivation behind these harmful online activities and furthermore highlight how they can become so addictive.

It's important to note that the victims of these acts may be prone to social media addiction, but they may also become addicted to the activities that victimize them. For example, someone who is being bullied online may feel terrible when they go online, but they can't stop themselves because they feel desperate to know what others are saying about them. Research indicates that, at least for teens, the more time spent online, the more likely the risk of getting cyberbullied. So, the Internet addict is at greater risk than the average person.

Research also shows that teens who experience cyberbullying are at greater risk of other addictions including substance misuse. Cyberbullying causes a number of problems and mental health issues; it's linked with depression, anxiety, and eating disorders as well as low self-esteem and self-harming behavior. These problems all put people at greater risk of addiction. This may manifest as addiction to social media specifically, Internet use generally, and/or to other behaviors or substances.

TEXTING ADDICTION

Not all relationship-related online addictions are to social media. Texting is another huge culprit. You don't even have to be connected to the Internet to text with people, although oftentimes you are. These days, it's hard to even define texting as separate from other forms of messaging. I have friends whom I know in real life who "text" me not only to my phone number but also through Facebook messenger and Instagram direct messages. The technology changes quickly; I used to chat privately with people on GChat and AOL, but I no longer use those applications. Snapchat and WeChat are two other major places where people "text" or send one-to-one messages to each other. So, for the purposes of this book, we'll loosely define a texting addiction as an addiction to sharing one-on-one private messages through any phone, computer, or other similar device.

Texting, even with someone you don't know, feels more personal than publicly commenting on social media. You're doing it privately (although sometimes in group texts), so it's got the sense of a new level of intimacy. This makes you feel more connected to the person on the other end of the message. Therefore, you place a higher value on their response. You text and your brain immediately starts to get excited for the response, seeking the dopamine hit of the reward of hearing from them. Sometimes you don't get the hit; you craft a carefully composed text message and get back just "ok" or "cool." That's not at all satisfying to the brain, so you immediately want to text again to see if you'll get a better reward.

Of course, just because you text frequently doesn't mean that you necessarily have an addiction. Dr. Kelly Lister-Landman did an interesting study into texting addiction, which found that teens differ by gender when it comes to texting addiction. Although boys and girls exchanged the same number of texts, the girls were significantly more likely to develop an addiction. In this study, addiction was characterized by trying to cut back on use but feeling unable to, getting frustrated by the behavior, and feeling defensive about their use. The boys weren't likely to have those problems, and although they texted often because of social norms, they could basically take it or leave it. In contrast, the girls had emotional attachments, and emotional consequences, associated with compulsive texting.

Many of the tools that we use to text offer addictive features. For example, there's the typing indicator; you can see that someone else is typing but hasn't yet sent the message because your device either tells you directly "typing" or shows you through symbols such as an ellipsis. You get anxious and excited for the response. Your brain is ready for that potential hit. Likewise, some services allow you to see that someone has read your message. How do you feel when someone reads what you wrote but hasn't yet responded? Do a million questions start going through your mind? Do you wonder what they're thinking and what you did "wrong" that made it so that they haven't responded yet? Does your worry cause you to want to text again?

Pairing text messaging with notifications can exacerbate addiction. In psychology, there's a well-recognized concept called classical conditioning. If you know the story about how Pavlov's dogs would salivate at the ringing of the bell, then you know about classical conditioning. Basically, you pair two things together (the dog hears the bell and then gets the food that he salivates over) and eventually just the first thing triggers the response (the dog hears the bell and begins salivating even if there's no food). Your text messages are probably paired with one or more triggers— a ping, a vibration, a notification number on the screen. You hear or see it, and you immediately start to have the feelings associated with the addiction. These days, you can choose from any number of different sounds to pair with your text messages, assigning different sounds to different people that you text with, and this increases your level of investment in the texting relationship so that you're even more easily triggered by those specific sounds.

Texting addiction can lead to physical problems—like text neck or texting thumb. It can lead to problems associated with lack of sleep due to waking up in the night to text. Texting during class can lead to problems at school; excessive or inappropriate texting at work can threaten your job. It's hard to say what amount of texts constitutes a problem, so it's important to consider the effects texting has on your social life, activities that you're passionate about, health and work performance, and so forth.

ADDICTION TO USE OF DATING APPS

Back in 1995, Match.com launched the first-ever commercial dating website. The people who paired up on Match back then could never even have envisioned what online dating would look like in the twenty-first century. There are hundreds of different dating sites and dating apps, some general and many niche. You can satisfy just about every interest you could possibly desire and connect with someone else who desires the same. "Connecting" with another person is as simple as swiping a finger across your phone. And with that prevalence and ease comes the increased likelihood of addiction.

The reasons, motivations, and problems associated with an addiction to dating apps are similar to those associated with other relationship-oriented Internet addictions including social media addictions. In fact, it's often directly tied in with other addictions. For example, you might have some selfie addiction or addiction to curating the perfect image as you try to present yourself to be the perfect dating material on different sites. You could become addicted to the "likes," constantly checking how many people are swiping positively for you. You might become addicted to looking at potential partners but never actually following through on dates. You could become addicted to the one-on-one messaging, including texting and sexting addiction. Or you could become addicted to short whirlwind relationships that you ultimately find unsatisfying, so you go back to your online connections.

In terms of harm, addiction to dating apps is most likely to cause problems in your current relationships. If you're in a relationship and "cheating" with dating apps, then that's an obvious trigger for problems. If you're single, then you might neglect your friendships and family in favor of your online dating world. Many dating apps are free, but some cost money, and of course going out on the dates costs money, so you might also develop negative consequences in your financial life as a result of dating app addiction. It can even lead to physical problems; just like there is texting thumb, there's also so-called Tinder Finger, which is pain in the index (or swiping) finger from constant, repetitive swiping on dating apps.

The problem of dating app addictions seems to be more prevalent than one might guess. One Match survey, reported on by VICE in 2017, found that one out of six single people feel addicted to the process of seeking out a partner online. Men are far more likely to feel addicted to it than women are, but women are more likely to report that the whole process makes them feel fatigued and even depressed. Dating app addiction may correlate with increased depression, anxiety, self-image issues, and low self-esteem.

ONLINE PORNOGRAPHY ADDICTION

Pornography addiction isn't necessarily the same as social media addiction, but it falls under the same umbrella in the sense that it is an online addictive behavior directly related to and impacting relationships with others. Compulsive behavior focused on online pornography is also known by the term "cybersexual addiction." We can see that it's on a spectrum with other social media addiction when we look at the similar term "cyber-relational addiction." This latter term refers to addiction to online relationships at the expense of relationships in real life, which describes any of the different types of addictions described in this chapter so far.

Along with gaming, pornographic content is considered one of the most potentially addictive content types available online. It is also one of the most widely studied behaviors of Internet addiction. It takes time for enough scientific studies to be done to really fully understand a mental health issue such as addiction; porn was one of the first popular content types on the Internet, so it has a long history available for study (or comparatively long anyway).

As such, this is a rich topic that really requires a full book to completely review and understand—and there are several of those books out there for people who are interested in the topic. Instead of digging that deep into it, we'll use what we already know about addiction in general, and Internet addiction specifically, to get a general grasp of online porn addictions. Specifically, let's recognize that porn has existed a lot longer than the Internet has and to take a look at what makes it much more likely to develop an online porn addiction than addiction to other types of porn.

This has to do directly with the technology itself, in particular the advances in that technology. Remember the story earlier in this book about how early games like those on the Atari system were naturally self-limiting in terms of addiction? No matter how exciting a single game was, it eventually got boring. And there were only so many games, so eventually you stopped playing Atari and did something else. Older versions of pornography are similar; you can only look through a single magazine so many times before the excitement is gone. Plus, the magazine is only a still image, so you have to utilize your imagination, stimulating other parts of your brain beyond just those that get addicted. The VHS tape or DVD porn movie uses a little bit less of your imagination, and it's a little bit more addictive, but eventually you've memorized it, and it no longer excites you.

But fast forward to pornography on the Internet today: there is virtually endless content of all types and varieties, and you can easily click from one to the next within seconds. You don't have to use your imagination at all because the Internet feeds you far more scenarios than you could imagine on your own. You passively consume the content, there's more and more of it, and you can easily see how this becomes much more addictive than the days when you had to covertly enter an adult bookstore to find the video that you'd watch for the next few weeks.

It's easy to see how online pornography feeds the brain's desire for intermittent reward. You click the video, and you may or may not like what you see. When you do, you get the dopamine reward. Online pornography also directly plays into the human desire for novelty. People follow a common trajectory starting out with "vanilla porn" and heading deeper and deeper into niche and kink porn. While there's nothing inherently wrong with a person's preference for a particular type of sex, Internet addiction can lead people to seek out more and more unique sex acts in the search for novelty. The desire to see more new things fuels more addictive behavior.

This has led to some disturbing issues, particularly for young people exposed to online pornography when their brains are still developing and their sexual desires still forming. Some people with addictions to Internet pornography find that real-life sexual experiences don't stimulate them because they feel dulled or muted in comparison with the intensity and click-click quickness of the online version of sex. They want to have sex with their partners in theory, but they can't get aroused or reach orgasm in the real world; yet, they have no trouble doing so with online porn. Even if you haven't experienced this yourself, you can easily imagine the many and varied problems that this can cause in relationships.

There's also the problem of desensitization to the other person when you do have real-life sexual relationships. Digital technology generally, and online pornography addiction specifically, may cause reduced empathy. If you don't recognize that the other person whom you're having sex with is a living, breathing, emotional human being, then you're at risk of causing a whole host of problems. At the very least, both of you leave the situation feeling a little bit empty, a little bit used, and very unsatisfied. Seeking a better feeling, the addict returns to porn and continues the cycle.

CHAPTER 5

Other Forms of Internet Addiction

Relationship-related forms of Internet addiction from social media to pornography represent very prevalent aspects of online addiction. Many aspects of that particular type of relational content are highly addictive. However, people get addicted to all different types of Internet content, some of which aren't relational at all. Gambling and media bingeing are just a few examples that we'll explore in this chapter.

GAMING ADDICTION

Like pornography, gaming straddles the line between being a solitary endeavor and one that's social. People can become addicted to very simple games that they play online, such as Solitaire or Mahjong. However, the most addictive games are also highly interactive with other players. Gaming addiction is one of the most widely studied forms of Internet addiction. As we've seen, it's the only form specifically listed in the *Diagnostic and Statistical Manual of Mental Disorders* (*DSM*) and *International Classification of Diseases* (*ICD*) as a mental health disorder.

Some games are more likely to provoke addiction than others. Low-risk games include puzzle games like *Tetris* and physical simulation games like *Guitar Hero*. Midrisk games include basic educational, historical context games and "God games" such as *The Sims*. Higher-risk games include role-playing games like *Legend of Zelda* as well as first person shooter games and real-time strategy games. The games that are most likely to activate addiction are the massive multiplayer online role-playing games (MMORPGs) including *RuneScape, EverQuest*, and *World of Warcraft*.

In fact, *World of Warcraft* is frequently cited as the most problematic game when it comes to gaming addiction. In its first ten years, the game gained more than one hundred million subscribers around the world. It received $10 billion in gross income. People immediately loved this game, and it became far more than just a fad; for many, it became an addiction.

In *World of Warcraft*, there are two warring factions called The Alliance and The Horde, constantly battling it out in a mythical land called Azeroth. Players create their own avatars, but they do not play alone. They join guilds to play in real time with other players from all around the world. Your guild is your team. Together you fight monsters, complete quests, and explore the virtual world. Whenever your guild-mates are online, you want to be online as well. You don't want them moving forward in the quest without you. This interactive nature enhances the addictive quality of games like *World of Warcraft*.

Interactivity and teaming up with others play right in to the brain's tendencies. Much like social media, this satisfies the desire for approval from others and the brain's urge to compare ourselves to others. Guild members can place a lot of peer pressure on one another to keep feeding the addiction, to stay online longer and skip other healthier, real-life activities. It's a primal instinct to want to fit in with the crowd. But these games prey upon other primal instincts as well.

These games feature some of the most highly distracting qualities of any online activity. They constantly send signals of sound, sight, and movement to the brain. Movement, in particular, puts the brain on high alert. Back when we humans had to hunt for our food and protect ourselves constantly from external threats, our brains learned to stay alert for movement. When we engage with these movement-rich, highly stimulating games, our brains remain in constant high alert. This messes with our adrenaline and cortisol as well as with the brain's neurotransmitters. We're constantly stressed, and this stress confuses the brain in ways that increase the risk of addiction.

Players may readily admit to having a gaming addiction, although that doesn't necessarily mean that they want to change their behavior. Author and gaming addiction expert Adam Alter reports that approximately half of the players in *World of Warcraft* consider themselves addicted to the game. In fact, there are online support groups specifically for people struggling with a *World of Warcraft* addiction. (Yes, there is some irony to an online group to help people stop online behavior, but it can be helpful, something we'll look at more in Chapter 9.) But recognizing that there's a problem doesn't necessarily lead people to seek help or to succeed in ending in an addiction.

At the extreme end of gaming addiction, players may experience gaming-induced psychosis. Of all the online activities that can addict people, gaming is the one most likely to cause this most severe of effects. One of the most common forms of this psychosis is called Game Transfer Phenomena (GTP). As the name suggests, it causes the player to have trouble separating the game from reality. It is sometimes called the *Tetris* effect, after the game of the same name, because addicted players may see *Tetris*-style patterns in the mind when not playing the game. Other symptoms of GTP include the experience of involuntary sensations and reacting physically and reflexively as though in game play even when the game is not on. Players may hear sounds or see images from the game when they are not playing.

GTP is typically a temporary, short-term effect that will go away with extended rest from the game. However, it can occasionally become a severe case of psychosis, especially if combined with sleep deprivation from game play. The more interactive and stimulating a game is, the more likely it is that addicted players will play for hours and hours straight without breaks. There are multiple known cases of people gaming for well over twenty-four hours without breaking to go to the bathroom or eat a snack. In severe cases, patients have had to go into inpatient treatment. They may spend weeks or even months there, away from the game, receiving therapy and medication, before they are fully back in the real world.

It is no accident that online gaming is addictive. The gaming industry, like the social media industry, wants people online all of the time, and they go to great lengths to make their games more and more addictive. Companies will conduct user studies that seem innocuous, but what they're really trying to figure out is how to make their games addictive. For example, they may measure a test subject's heart rate during different stages of game play to learn how to get the heart rate going more effectively. Companies hire people from fields including psychology and neurobiology to further strengthen their ability to make games addictive. They prey upon what we know about human addiction to make the games addictive.

The result is an impact not only on behavior but also on the brain. In a 2001 study from the Indiana School of Medicine, researchers found that the brain changed after just one week of playing violent video games. Compared to a sample group that did not play the games, players who gamed for ten hours in one week had decreased activation in both the left interior frontal lobe and the anterior cingulate cortex. These are the areas of the brain that help to control emotion and aggression. That's ten hours in one week; today's gaming addict is more likely to exceed ten hours in one day.

So far, we haven't talked much about aggression, but it's another problematic side effect of some online addictions and is particularly prevalent among people who play violent video games. In the same way that an addiction to online pornography can desensitize the person to sex, addiction to violent gaming can desensitize a person to violence. Studies show that immediately after playing a violent game, people are more likely to show aggressive behavior and less likely to feel affected by violence around them.

Not only does violent gaming beget desensitization but violence in a game increases the likelihood of addiction as well. A study by author Jennifer Burek Pierce compared teenagers playing violent and nonviolent action games. The results found that in comparison the teens who played violent games had

- increased activation in the amygdala, which means that they were more emotionally aroused;
- decreased activation in the prefrontal areas of the brain correlated with focus and control; and
- increased feeling of fight-or-flight.

These results happened whether they won the game, lost the game, or even paused the game in the middle. The effects continued even after game play ended. All of these changes in brain activity make a game more addictive.

In the current age, there is also another motivation for gaming addiction, which is that top-level players now have celebrity status. There is an entire genre of gaming called eSports, and people tune in to watch the masters at play. Regular gamers may strive to become a celebrity player, and the only way to do that is to practice excessively. They work hard to get the slightest edge over other players. For example, they will tweak their hand and arm positions to attempt to get just a fraction more speed in a game. They play and play and play. The more they play, the more they want to play, and thus an addiction can form.

NET COMPULSIONS: GAMBLING, AUCTIONS, AND MORE

Net compulsions refer to a variety of activities that addicts engage in repeatedly and obsessively. There is a fine line between addiction and compulsion in psychology. Compulsion, often but not always associated with obsessive compulsive disorder, is defined by a fear-based need to engage in specific behaviors. Compulsion is often one component of addictive behavior; the addict feels a compulsive need to keep checking on something or engaging in a behavior. An addict with a net compulsion may feel a constant need to check on the status of an online auction or the newest clearance items available on a site like Amazon. They may also feel the need to keep going back to a site, such as an online gambling site.

Gambling is actually the only behavioral addiction that's officially defined as a problem by the *DSM*-5. This is separate from online addiction and refers to people with an addiction to gambling of any kind. In the twenty-first century, gambling can now take place online, leading to potential addictive behavior both online and offline. In other words, someone with a gambling problem may or may not have an Internet addiction; someone addicted to gambling online has an Internet addiction.

Interestingly, gambling in the real world preys upon many of the same brain weaknesses that we've discussed with regard to Internet addiction. The people who design casinos, for example, have taken a variety of psychological and neurological factors into play to increase a person's tendencies toward addiction. The sounds of slot machines, the placement of tables in a casino, and the carefully controlled temperature—no part of the design is left to chance. In the same way that social media companies and video game designers try to get you to stay online longer, casinos try to get you to keep spending your money as long as possible. Video game designers have studied the casinos' playbooks and implemented their most successful strategies.

So, it's no surprise that online gambling is potentially addictive. These days you can bet online on everything from the outcome of a sports game to the gender of a celebrity's next baby. Jarice Hanson reported that as of 2007, there were more than $14 billion globally in the world of online gambling. Also, of great importance, the author explains that people who are already addicted to some other aspect of the Internet are much more likely to become addicted to Internet gambling. If you have an addiction to social media or video games and you stumble into online gambling, then you're at risk of addiction.

There are a lot of legal issues related to online gambling, which vary significantly from location to location. Online gaming website owners constantly change their tactics in order to be able to continue operating. For example, one law says that there's nothing illegal about a U.S. resident placing an online bet as long as it's on a site that itself is located in a different country, so gambling sites are typically hosted outside of the United States, but U.S. users can access them. There is a lot of money at stake here, and people are willing to go above and beyond to keep these sites up.

Online gambling is only one of many possible net compulsions though. Two of the other most common examples are online stock trading and participating in online auctions. These activities keep you online at all hours of the day and night, constantly checking and updating your activity. If you want to win the eBay auction, then you might set your alarm to remind you right before the auction is about to end so that you can stop whatever else you might be doing and get online to make some rush bids. Although it's possible to automate many of these activities, the addict thrives on the rush of the compulsive behavior.

People can develop net addictions to all different types of content. Just a few more examples include the following:

- Compulsively clipping online coupons and looking for the best deal
- Regularly returning to a website that sells items to check for new products and better prices
- Participating in online surveys and entering giveaways

In addition to all of the common consequences of any Internet addiction, people with net compulsions are those most likely to experience financial consequences. Many of the net compulsions involve spending money, whether that's on gambling or shopping. As a result, people with this form of addiction often end up in extreme debt.

ADDICTION TO INTERNET MEDIA

People can become addicted to any specific type of content, whether that's pornography, gaming, or gambling. They can also become addicted to specific types of media that are available online. Streaming video, news, and health information are among the most problematic content types ripe for addiction.

Television (The Netflix Binge)

One of the most fascinating changes in technology has been how seamlessly media now moves from one device to the next. For example, people used to watch all of their television on a TV set. However, in modern times, a person may access the same television show on their desktop, laptop, tablet, or phone. The devices are often synced so that you can pause a show on one device and pick up right where you left off using another device. Advances in streaming technology have made it possible to easily watch "live tv" on the go.

Netflix offers one of the best examples of a company that has changed with the times. The business emerged at a time when brick-and-mortar DVD and VHS stores such as Blockbuster were going out of business. Netflix created a mail-order service that allowed people to get DVDs sent right to their homes. The online component at that time was that you had an account where you looked for the videos that you wanted, set them up in a queue, and ordered them for home delivery. However, the technology continued to change rapidly, and it wasn't too long before they launched their streaming service to watch television and movies directly on the website. They went on to create their own content, and those Netflix Originals are now some of the most popular streaming content.

As far as Internet addiction goes, the most relevant thing has been the emergence of the phenomenon of "binge watching." Even the term itself suggests that this is a disordered behavior. After all, nobody typically thinks of "bingeing" as a positive thing. And yet, the phrase rapidly was adopted by people who regularly tell others about their viewing binges without any shame or concern. We use it regularly in everyday parlance. We don't seem that concerned about the Netflix binge.

Obviously, you can binge any streaming TV/movie content; it doesn't have to be on Netflix. Netflix just cornered the early market on the binge through smart choices that preyed upon the brain's addictive nature. The design of the website, feeding you content that you might be interested in while also allowing you to collect your own content in your queue, is one of those smart choices. They were also brilliant when they first started releasing entire seasons of their own original content at one time. One of the early examples was *Orange Is the New Black*; new fans of the show did not have to wait from one week to the next to find out what would happen but instead could watch the whole first season (and then subsequent seasons) in just a day or two. We now see this model replicated across many different platforms, of which Netflix is only one.

Any type of content can become ripe for binge watching. In particular, content featuring real people (reality TV or docuseries) and content with fictional characters that you can really relate to are ripe for bingeing. What these have in common is that they provide an illusion that the characters are real people who viewers can get to know. In some cases, they are real people (like the Kardashians), but they are exaggerated and edited versions of those real people. This content is addictive in that the viewer constantly wonders what will happen next with the character. "Just one more episode" has become a common refrain in this society. The addict simply can't stop, often foregoing sleep and socialization for that next episode.

This plays to the voyeur in people, to the point where some become more comfortable viewing lives on the screen than interacting with people in real life. They use the characters to replace real companionship. However, these one-sided relationships are ultimately unsatisfying. Therefore, the addict needs to watch more and more online television to get that same feeling of "connection." They may participate in online discussions and fan groups and also follow the celebrity's social media accounts to get even more time "with" them.

Online News Addiction

There once was a time, not all that long ago, when the day's news was only available for an hour or so per day, with different versions across three or four channels. Then along came cable television and the start of the twenty-four-hour news cycle. You could tune into news all day long, getting different versions from various news anchors. It became addictive content. The addictive nature has only heightened now that news is available online. It's always at our fingertips.

Online news comes in various formats. You can access mainstream news through online streaming services. You can view alternative points of view on various sites including YouTube channels. Add in podcasts, vlogs, blogs, and social media, and there is a never-ending stream of news that you can tune into at any time. In fact, with social media at play, it has become increasingly difficult not to be exposed to news, even if you aren't actively seeking it. People constantly post and repost "news" based on an article's headlines so that anytime you're looking at your social media feed, there are items in there designed to capture your attention.

People become addicted to news for a variety of reasons. Fear of missing out (FOMO) is one big one. The addict insists that it's important to stay on top of our society's news and worries and that if they aren't constantly checking it, then they are going to miss out on important information. There's also an addictive quality to the feelings that news stirs up in us. Much of the news out there is "bad" news that produces fear and anxiety, and the addict has a compulsion to keep checking that news, perhaps hoping for something better but becoming addicted to the chemicals of fear that the headlines evoke.

Fitness Apps/Wearable Tech

Technology changes as fast as humans can come up with new ideas. Wearable tech is a relatively new technology that is already fairly pervasive in our society. People use smart watches, fitness tracker accessories, and apps on their cell phones to constantly monitor their own activity. On its own, there is nothing wrong with this technology. However, it creates one more way that we can become addicted to the Internet.

Specifically, this type of technology can lead to or enhance an exercise addiction. Apps constantly remind you of your activity so that you can consistently push yourself further and further in exercise. Someone who is already prone to guilt over inactivity may pass the tipping point when faced with a device that constantly reminds them of it. This can lead to self-destructive behaviors, such as pushing through an injury just to meet a goal and get that positive feedback from the app.

The "online" component makes this technology more addictive. Many of these tools don't merely provide you with information about your own body. Instead, they also connect you to a community of peers. The idea is to provide accountability for exercise. However, it also means that you constantly have an audience, and you may feel like they are judging you on your performance. You may feel that you have to tune in and perform despite messages from your body that what you are doing is not healthy. Alerts from the devices combined with social interactivity prime you for addiction.

Cyberchondria

Exercise is just one type of health behavior that is ripe for online addiction. Another related content type is medical information. Perhaps you have experienced something like this; you have a pimple on your arm that won't go away, and you have recently had a headache. These things are probably unrelated, and both will likely go away soon. However, you get curious, so you start searching online for medical advice as to what might be "wrong" with you.

You aren't alone. Larry Rosen reports on a Pew Center study that found that searching for medical or health information is the third-most popular Internet activity behind only more general Internet searches and use of email. More than 80 percent of people search for information on health websites. So, you think that you might have something wrong with you, and you do a search. Before you know it, you are deep in an Internet hole, concerned that you might have a rare condition characterized by these two traits. Most people are eventually able to pull themselves away from the Internet and settle down, realizing that they are just scaring themselves over nothing. However, some people get addicted to researching this type of information, and they can develop a condition called cyberchondria.

Cyberchondria is a specific form of anxiety caused by looking up health-related information online. Although it is most common for people to research this medical information about their own symptoms, occasionally the anxiety arises when doing Internet searches to assist friends and family members; in such a case, the term for the condition is "cyberchondria by proxy." The condition is a terrific example of how normal human behavior becomes amplified and exaggerated online, which can lead to a dangerous increase in the symptoms of certain psychological conditions, with the potential for serious physical health consequences that follow.

Cyberchondria stems from our brain's natural tendency to consider the "worst case scenario" for potentially dangerous situations. This tendency is reasonable when considered from an evolutionary perspective. Using this adaptive tool allows us to predict danger and make choices to avoid it. For example, when we are walking at night and see that the street lights are out up ahead, we consider that there could be a mugger hiding in the shadows and adapt our route accordingly. Chances are there is no mugger, but our minds let us know of this outlier risk to prevent even the small chance of harm. In such an example, the brain has given us enough warning that we quickly identify the cause of our anxiety and make a shift that alleviates the anxiety. Unfortunately, this is the same part of the brain that gets triggered in cyberchondria, but the actions that we take in response actually increase our anxiety instead of quelling it.

Instead of pointing out the worst-case scenario and providing a means of escaping it, the online medical search highlights this scenario in such a way that we are drawn ever toward it. Imagine that you have a hoarse voice and a sore throat, and you initiate a web search to find out what might be wrong with you. Scanning the results of your search, you guess that the most likely culprit is all of the yelling you were doing at a concert the night before. However, before you turn off the screen, you notice that cancerous tumors in the throat also have the same symptoms. Your mind seeks to resolve anxiety over this worst-case scenario, so you dig to find additional information. With just a few clicks, you become convinced that you might actually have a tumor. You spend the entire night awake and terrified, rushing to your doctor first thing in the morning. The doctor assures you that it is unlikely to be a tumor, but your brain recalls all of the information from the Internet search and insists that you complete a wide variety of medical tests to be sure. The tumor is as unlikely as the mugger in the shadows, but there is no relief from taking another route home; treating the hoarse throat doesn't rule out the tumor.

Cyberchondria itself is a challenging psychological condition. As with all forms of anxiety, it exists on a spectrum from mild to severe.

Symptoms can range from being tired after a sleepless night of Internet searches to persistent fight-or-flight response in the body that causes muscle pain, migraines, and other physical ailments as well as changes in brain chemistry. This creates a vicious cycle; worrying that you are sick makes you sick.

Cyberchondria also has a number of additional consequences for both individuals and the greater community. The prevalence of this condition has led to a significant increase in the number of people visiting their doctors and a corresponding increase in the number of tests run on patients. This puts a strain on the medical system, which frustrates doctors, increases office waiting times for people with serious medical conditions, and raises insurance rates. People subject themselves to invasive procedures, including extensive surgeries, to treat their "medical issues," all in a futile attempt to alleviate their own anxiety. This exacerbates physical symptoms that reinforce the belief that they are ill. Chronic pain, gastrointestinal dress, and cardiovascular symptoms are all common among people who believe that they are sick. Additionally, there is an increase in likelihood of depression.

Cyberchondria is an example of how the brain's normal adaptive functions get derailed when interacting with technology. A fascinating sidebar to this is that our human behaviors teach computers to behave in a way that further exacerbates our anxiety. Computer search algorithms are designed to gather information about what humans search for in order to predict "better" search results for the next person. The problem with online medical searches is that the average person will be more drawn to find out about the tumor than the classic sore throat. Each time that a person clicks on the "tumor," the computer records that this is the "better" response and feeds more information about tumors to people who are searching for information on hoarse throats. This leads an ever-increasing number of people to consider this worst-case medical scenario. Computer search engineers have been working on this issue, and changes are slowly being made to the technology to help combat the growth of cyberchondria. In the meantime, it is up to each individual to use common sense and sound in-person medical consultation to battle the anxiety that wells up every time a potential new "symptom" seems to manifest in the body. However, the more you indulge the urge to do this search, the more likely you are to fall prey to an addiction to keep doing it.

Searching for health information isn't the only issue. There are so many different ways that we receive medical information from our devices these days. There are advertisements and commercials telling us about various heretofore-unheard-of conditions and recommending specific medications.

Every streaming video option has some sort of medical-related television show. Even just posting on social media can become a problem because when you share that you are ill, others immediately sympathize, and that in itself can become addictive.

So, as you can see from the past two chapters, there are many aspects of the Internet that can provoke addiction. When you fall prey to one specific addiction, you may change your brain in such ways that make you susceptible to other online addictions.

CHAPTER 6

At-Risk Populations

As with all addiction, anybody can be at risk of Internet addiction. However, some people are more susceptible to it than others. One of the things that are particularly important to understand in terms of the neuroscience of addiction is that at this point in scientific research, we often aren't able to differentiate cause from effect. We don't have the means to know whether someone first becomes addicted and that causes changes in the brain or whether they already started out with certain structural and chemical brain issues that primed them to become addicted. It's likely a combination of both. With that in mind, let's take a look at some of the populations that seem to be most at risk of developing an Internet addiction.

CHILDREN AND TEENS

People who were born before the ubiquity of the Internet may be at greater risk of Internet addiction than those who were born before its widespread common use. Gen Z, and to a large extent latter-born millennials, began using devices at a young age. Because they don't know anything else, they may be more susceptible to the Internet's risks of addiction. More than that, though, we know that Internet use and misuse can change the brain, and we know that children's brains are still in development, so although we don't exactly know how these two things are going to play out over time, we can guess that people growing up with Internet use are going to have a different neurochemical balance than previous generations. This might be primed for addiction.

The brains of children and teens are still in development, and thus they are even more susceptible to habit-forming input than the adult brain. Put simply, children's brains aren't well equipped to handle the intense level of stimulation caused by constant computer use. That dopamine hit is strong! In fact, the teen brain actually receives more of a dopamine hit than the adult brain does for the same activity. Therefore, it loves to seek out the constant rewards of the Internet. The brain easily habituates to that dopamine increase. Dopamine plays such a key role in addiction that it's likely to place young brains at risk.

We discussed some brain anatomy in Chapter 3, including the important role that the prefrontal cortex and frontal lobe play in uniquely human characteristics. This area of the brain, which helps control impulsivity, is not yet fully formed in teens. Thus, teens notably already have trouble with impulse control. Their brains literally can't do it yet. Teens who spend a significant amount of time on the Internet may inhibit the development of the frontal cortex, further reducing their ability to develop impulse control. So, they don't have the control to stop themselves from the compulsive Internet behaviors in the first place, and then engaging in those behaviors makes them less likely to develop the brain's ability to control their impulses.

A teen's natural brain changes happen to be well suited to the kinds of technological habits that modern society encourages, habits that can lead to addiction. For example, have you ever noticed that teens love to stay up late at night? This isn't just a social drive; it's a drive in the teen brain. Adolescence resets the teen's circadian rhythm so that biologically they are driven to stay up later and then sleep in. What can a teen do in the middle of the night if they aren't allowed to leave the house? The obvious answer is to use their phone or computer. The brain embraces a sleep pattern that encourages the teen to stay up, plus it seeks out that dopamine stimulation, and the Internet is the perfect solution.

Moreover, choices made during this stage of brain development can have a lifelong impact on a person's patterns. You see, there are certain periods of life when the brain is particularly malleable. In other words, the information you put in at that time will stick more readily than if you learn the same information at another time. That's why it's easier to learn a second language when you are young, particularly at certain stages of brain development. This relates to neuroplasticity; younger brains are more malleable than older brains. However, there are also specific developmental stages during which brains are especially malleable. Right around the time that we learn to speak (ages one to two) and again in our teen years, our brains are very open to change.

Teens go through a period during which there is heightened malleability. It usually happens just before puberty, and it's the brain's last big burst of sensitivity to growth. Basically, whatever patterns the brain takes on at that time are likely going to form neural pathways that create habits that can last a lifetime. Therefore, if a teen starts to learn an instrument at that time, they will probably always have some proclivity toward skill with that instrument. However, the brain doesn't discriminate; whatever information and patterns you put in at this time are what will stick. So, if the teen spends all of their time playing video games or surfing the web, those are the patterns that will be strengthened. Of course, change is always possible, but it becomes increasingly difficult once those patterns are wired into the brain.

Whatever the teen's time is focused on, that's where the pathways will develop. If the teen is hyperfocused on Internet use, it will be at the expense of other brain development. For example, the brain chemicals and structure of the teen brain are perfectly primed to learn and develop problem-solving skills that will help them all throughout life. However, this needs to be developed, practiced, and maintained in order to become a natural path for the brain. If instead the teen is distracted by the immediacy of the Internet, they might not develop those skills. The less developed the brain, the more prone it can be to addictive behavior.

As for younger children, there is a lot of debate about how much and what kind of screen time to allow at different ages. There is widespread agreement that screen time, including traditional TV time, is detrimental to the brain growth and development of young children. The American Academy of Pediatrics warns against allowing younger than age two to consume media. And yet, as many as nine out of ten kids under two years old do have screen time, plus they're regularly exposed to the "background noise" of screens in use by others around them. We don't know if this makes them more likely to become addicted. We do not know that it can impact their development particularly as it relates to language development and early social skills, and if those get damaged, then the brain may react in ways that make addiction more likely.

Of equal importance as the potential damage of screen time is the fact that if children are excessively engaged with Internet devices, then they are not engaged with some of the most important things that they need in order to grow and develop healthy brains and healthy relationships. The more time they spend on their screens, the less time they spend in human interaction, downtime daydreaming, and experiences out in nature, all of which are critical to human development. According to Attention Restoration Theory (an idea first posited in the 1980s by Rachel and Stephen Kaplan), spending downtime in nature has a restorative effect that helps humans to heal. Nature time improves attention, emotion, social interaction, and stress reduction in humans. Humans who do not spend time in nature aren't getting this all-important restoration.

The reality is that kids today are growing up with screens, both at home and at school. Some use of those devices probably doesn't cause any major problem or lead the average child into addiction. But more frequent use, and use of more stimulating content, might become problematic, particularly for very young children. Certain children may also just be more sensitive than others. We don't know. If that's a topic that you're interested in learning about in more depth, Anya Kamenetz's book *The Art of Screen Time*, designed particularly for parents, is a balanced starting place about the current research. What we do know is that children and teens have developing brains, the Internet does interact with the brain, and as we continue to learn more and more about Internet addiction, we have to pay particular attention to risks for youth.

INDIVIDUALS WITH ATTENTION DEFICIT HYPERACTIVITY DISORDER

The relationship between attention deficit hyperactivity disorder (ADHD) and addiction to the Internet is complicated. ADHD can be a risk factor for Internet addiction. On the other hand, traits of Internet addiction can look a lot like ADHD. It is hard to separate out cause and effect in a world where ADHD is on the rise and Internet use is prevalent. We simply don't know why there has been an increase in diagnosis of ADHD, and it's possible that increased technology could play a role in how many more people experience the symptoms of the condition. To complicate things even further, there are traits about ADHD that make Internet addiction more appealing, but we can't generally parse out which issue came first.

One important thing to understand is that ADHD is a medical condition, one that is specifically related to the brain. As the brain interacts with the world around it, ADHD can be triggered or exacerbated. This isn't to say that Internet use causes ADHD; we don't know that. However, it might increase the development or severity of symptoms in some people because of the way that it interacts with the brain.

Consider, for example, how frequent Internet use impacts the brain in terms of that dopamine hit. You want more and more stimulation. The brain seeking stimulation like that looks very much like the ADHD brain. We don't have enough information, yet, to determine whether technology can cause ADHD. However, there is enough information to suggest that further study is required.

Of more immediate importance, perhaps, is that research does indicate that people who do have an ADHD diagnosis are at greater risk of developing an Internet addiction. Pediatric neurologist Martin L. Kutscher reports that someone with an ADHD diagnosis has a 25 percent risk of developing an addiction to the Internet. In fact, studies indicate that there are differences in the ADHD brain that naturally make addictive behavior more likely. Of course, this includes addiction to Internet usage.

Furthermore, people with ADHD already have a difficult time focusing, and the Internet provides ample opportunity for continuous distraction. Specifically, people with addiction tend to have reduced activity in the prefrontal brain regions, which is also lower among people with ADHD. Even people with terrific focus find Internet multitasking to be very tempting. The ADHD brain has a very low tolerance for routine; it gets bored quickly. Therefore, it's especially prone to finding new things to do online.

Video games, in particular, can become addictive, because constantly changing games offer consistent opportunities for novel stimulation. ADHD is a condition that relates to attention, but remember that the brain has different kinds of attention. Top-down attention is voluntary; it's when we actively make ourselves focus on something. That's very hard for the ADHD brain. Then there's the attention that just grabs us, activating our more primal instincts that look out for movement and other sensory stimuli. The ADHD brain has no problem with that kind of attention, so a child with ADHD may be able to spend hours on a video game despite attention issues they experience when engaging with more analog activities.

INDIVIDUALS WITH AUTISM SPECTRUM DISORDERS

Autism spectrum disorders (ASD), including Asperger's, also place people—particularly children with the condition—at a greater risk of Internet addiction. Autism manifests in many different ways, and there are also related conditions, including sensory processing disorder, that we are still learning more and more about each day. However, to simplify things, there are two basic issues that people with ASD have

1. trouble with communication and social interaction including challenges with nonverbal communication, understanding social cues, sharing emotions with others, and forming strong relationships;
2. a narrow range of interests and/or behaviors including repetitive moments, intense focus on just a few passionate subjects, and decreased sensitivity to certain stimuli.

Laura James, writing in *Odd Girl Out*, shares more about how people on the autism spectrum often have special interests. Not only are they pleasurable but special interests also help provide a sense of identity and self-esteem for many people with ASD. In some cases, the special interest becomes an obsession, where they tend toward destructiveness. The Internet can become part of this destructiveness. James shares that this was the case for her when two major political elections became the subject of her special interest. She couldn't tear herself away from the news, and she supplemented it 24/7 with Twitter and Facebook updates, causing a variety of problems in her life. She decided to take a Twelve Steps approach—one minute at a time—to get herself off of political social media. To clarify, she developed the obsession as part of her autism—it was her special interest—but the obsessive destructiveness was facilitated by the constant availability of information from various Internet channels. She developed an addiction to the Internet as a result of her desire to find information about her special interest.

Furthermore, specific Internet activities can themselves become objects of special interests; someone can become passionately interested in a specific video game or a specific website, for example. Kevin Roberts reports that in treating children on the spectrum, he has found particularly high levels of addiction to video games. Not only do the kids with ASD tend to play more than others but they also seem to get much more physically involved with the game than the average players. Heavy breathing, jerking legs, and body gyrations are all common among the kids whom he sees.

This isn't to say that Internet use is all bad when it comes to people with ASD. In fact, much about the Internet is actually helpful for people with ASD, which can complicate things, and which we'll explore more in Chapter 9. On the one hand, it can be good for them, and on the other hand, it could make them more prone to an Internet addiction.

In a glance at the good stuff, one example is that people with nonverbal forms of autism may be able to communicate through the use of technological devices that provide them with a voice. Even people with ASD who are verbal may find it challenging to communicate well with others. The opportunity to respond in writing online, and taking the time to do so, helps facilitate socialization for some people. However, it is sometimes used as an alternative, rather than an adjunct, to communication and socialization. In other words, sometimes people on the autism spectrum avoid real-life situations because they are uncomfortable. This means that they don't get the practice necessary to improve in-person communication, thus reinforcing the awkwardness and leading to increased isolation.

This is a particular risk for children on the spectrum. So, the Internet can be helpful or harmful, but this is definitely an at-risk population.

MILITARY MEMBERS AND VETERANS

Anyone who has experienced trauma is at risk of Internet addiction. Trauma is often correlated with overactivity in the amygdala, which affects dopamine levels, and as we know, that can lead to increased likelihood of Internet addiction. People in the military have often experienced trauma, and therefore, they are at risk.

In particular, military veterans often find themselves addicted to video games, especially violent ones. There is one famous, unfortunate case, of a veteran named Aaron Alexis. He was a video gamer addicted to *Call of Duty*, which is a violent shooting game. He would play for upwards of sixteen hours each day, often sacrificing sleep in order to play. He became delusional, went out into the real world, and killed twelve people.

Of course, most veterans won't go shoot people in civilian life. Most won't even become delusional despite prolonged, addictive play. However, their experiences with firearms, plus the trauma that affects their brain chemistry, can make shooter games especially appealing to this population. While first person shooter games aren't quite as addictive as massive multiplayer online role-playing games (MMORPGs), they do have addictive properties that people can fall prey to. The military has been actively studying Internet and gaming addiction in recent years, and it's an area worthy of further study.

SOCIALLY ISOLATED INDIVIDUALS

Author Johann Hari did a TED talk in which he says, "The opposite of addiction is connection." Addiction feeds on loneliness and isolation. Therefore, anyone who experiences social isolation for any reason at all can be at risk of addiction in general. In fact, there is a well-known study called Rat Park that clearly demonstrates that isolation leads to addiction.

This study built upon earlier studies into drug addiction. In the earlier studies, rats were placed in solitary confinement inside of boxes where they couldn't see or touch other rats. They were never let out of their cages, and they had very little stimulation from their human caregivers. The rats were able to press a lever that would inject them with drugs. The initial studies found that the rats would regularly dose themselves, consuming large amounts of heroin, cocaine, and other drugs. At the time, the information was used to suggest that rats, and by extension humans, just love drugs and can't help themselves.

However, a group of researchers at Simon Fraser University decided to test this theory, in what became known as Rat Park. They created a relatively normal environment for the rats, one where they could live together, socializing and enjoying a variety of activities. It was called Rat Park because they had playground-like toys to play with, plus they had each other. Many variations were made to the situation during the research, but basically, the social rats were compared to those in solitary confinement. Regardless of the other variables, the social rats always consumed far fewer drugs than those who were locked up alone. When given the opportunity to interact with others, they apparently didn't feel the need for the drugs. Put the other way, rats in isolation numbed out with drugs, because they felt lonely or bored or both.

This is just one study that has shown that social isolation increases risk of addiction in general. The Internet offers faux social connection plus ongoing distraction, making it a richly potential source for addiction. And there are so many people that this can impact, people who feel socially isolated for so many different reasons. Illness that leaves people homebound, old age, living in a rural community, or simply not fitting in can all lead people to feel like they are alone.

As we saw earlier in the book, loneliness is also a symptom or side effect of Internet addiction. So, it's another of those Catch-22, chicken-and-egg problems. People who are already socially isolated are more likely to develop an addiction, and the addiction itself can increase the feeling of loneliness. The more you use your devices to reduce loneliness, the less you feel comfortable socializing in the real world; the more you turn to the Internet, the lonelier you actually feel. It is self-reinforcing. The Internet becomes a coping mechanism.

For example, Kevin Roberts describes a client who had a gaming addiction. He intended to quit, and he made every effort to do so, in large part by going out into the world to socialize. However, going out into the world triggered his social anxiety, making him feel even more isolated even though he was technically out with others. He would get overwhelmed, go home, and turn to his gaming addiction to soothe that anxiety.

MENTAL HEALTH AND SUBSTANCE USE ISSUES

People living with mental health issues may be at increased risk of Internet addiction for a variety of reasons. The aforementioned social isolation is one cause, because despite increased awareness, there is still much stigma associated with many of these conditions. Another big factor is the interplay of brain chemistry with addictive tendencies. Each condition, and each person with that condition, has different specific brain chemistry issues to consider. However, generally speaking, any mental health issue can make someone more prone to Internet addiction. We'll discuss this in more depth in Chapter 8, on comorbidity.

One specific diagnosis of particular concern worth mentioning here is that of schizoid disorder. This is a type of personality disorder, which is characterized in part by emotional detachment and a strong desire to be alone. This drive toward low socialization increases the potential attraction of the Internet. The research into this connection is still very new. However, one study from California State University (CSU) Dominguez Hills has shown a direct correlation between schizoid personality disorder and high levels of media use. The correlation is particularly strong in younger people.

Another type of mental health issue worth discussing here is that of substance use. Anyone who has an active addiction to drugs or alcohol is at greater risk of developing other addictions including Internet addiction. Moreover, people who are in recovery for substance addiction are at particularly high risk of developing Internet addiction.

Nicholas Kardaras shares in his introduction to the book *Glow Kids* that he's a recovering addict. He notes that despite being in recovery for many years and being an expert in this field, he finds it increasingly difficult to maintain a healthy relationship with his own smartphone. Since technology triggers the same responses in the brain as drugs, it is especially important for addicts in recovery to be vigilant about the impact that their Internet use may have. People who are in recovery for behavioral addictions (e.g., compulsive gambling) are also more at risk of developing Internet addiction.

Put simply, some people are just more predisposed to addiction than other people are. They crave that dopamine hit more than the rest of us. Therefore, even though a person is in recovery doesn't mean that they lose that craving. Instead, they learn coping mechanisms to fight the craving. This can sometimes lead to cross-addiction, which is substituting one addiction for another. Someone with an addiction history certainly doesn't look at the Internet and think it will have the same effects as the drug. Nevertheless, Internet use might creep up as part of a recovery coping mechanism. It's another, safer—or at least legal—way to get a similar feeling.

SPECIFIC TRAITS THAT MIGHT MAKE A PERSON SUSCEPTIBLE TO ADDICTION

In addition to all of the risk factors cited in this chapter, here are some specific traits that might increase the risk of Internet addiction:

- Desire for escape
- Disorganization and lack of conscientiousness
- Emotional volatility and mood swings
- Family history of addiction
- High need for novelty
- Identity crisis or instability
- Impulsive behavior
- Introversion
- Limited range of coping skills
- Low self-esteem
- Negative situations in life
- Problems with attention span
- Problems with anger and aggression
- Risk-taking behavior
- Social deviance
- Stress and/or trauma

Anytime that we talk about risk factors, we also have to talk about protective factors. In other words, someone may have a lot of traits that make them susceptible to an Internet addiction, but if they have enough protective factors, then they might be less likely to develop that addiction. Protective factors for Internet addiction include high-quality family and friend relationships, maintaining active engagement with non-Internet hobbies and activities, and intentionally placing limitations on the duration of Internet use.

PART II

Issues and Controversies

CHAPTER 7

Treatment Options

Internet addiction is a problem. It exists on a spectrum, and many of us find ourselves exhibiting some symptoms on that spectrum today even though we don't have a true addiction. And, of course, there are the extreme cases of Internet addiction at the other end of the spectrum: the people whose lives are ruined because of their Internet activities. People at different parts of the spectrum may find that different treatments are most effective. Luckily, there are a variety of treatment options available to help deal with Internet addiction.

Because Internet addiction is new in our society, these treatment options are relatively new. In some cases, they're old methods (like talk therapy) adapted to the new condition. Either way, they're controversial. Some people swear by one and don't believe in the others. Others don't believe that Internet addiction is a problem requiring treatment at all. Despite the controversy, what's true is that there are some people out there struggling with what they perceive to be an Internet addiction, and there are different treatment options that may or may not help those individuals.

HARM REDUCTION

In the world of addiction, there are two primary treatment paths. The first is total abstinence. This is often used in treating drug addiction, where the goal is to stop using the drug immediately, entirely, and forever. The second path is harm reduction. This is common in treating food addiction, where the goal would obviously not be to never eat food again but instead to develop a healthy relationship with eating, reducing harm caused by food consumption.

Since we live in a constantly connected world, it doesn't make sense to aim for Internet abstinence. After all, what would happen if you went to your school or job and told them that you could no longer use computers? Therefore, the Internet addiction treatment goal instead is harm reduction. The idea is to learn to use Internet devices in intentional, limited ways for the person's benefit without falling back into addictive behavior. In some cases, this may mean abstinence from specific Internet activities, such as online pornography or video games.

It may also mean abstinence or "detox" for a period of time. Sometimes a person with an Internet addiction does have to quit all forms of Internet activity until they have successfully cut ties with their addiction. Only then can they start to use the Internet again in limited ways that are less destructive. Although there may be some treatment providers out there that recommend complete and permanent Internet abstinence for addicts, that approach is extreme and not well suited to today's connected society, so all of the options in this book are harm reduction treatments.

PLACES TO RECEIVE INTERNET ADDICTION TREATMENT

Where should you go if you want to get help for an Internet addiction? There are a wide variety of options. In fact, the options are increasing rapidly as more and more people recognize the problem of addiction as well as the general value of disconnecting at times from the Internet. As with any addiction, there is no one-size-fits-all treatment plan. The approach needs to be individualized to the client's specific needs.

A person might need to try several different treatment options before they find the one that is the perfect match. Some people find that even if a specific type of treatment doesn't "work" (meaning it doesn't entirely break the addiction), it can lend value, increasing insight in ways that lead to reduction in the behaviors. The takeaway is that people with Internet addiction may need to try several different approaches, but there is no harm in ones that appear at first to "fail" because they add to the personal growth process and aid in harm reduction over time.

Rehab Centers

One of the most popular, and most intense, Internet addiction treatment options is inpatient rehab. These centers restrict or entirely cut off Internet connection. This gives the person a chance to completely disconnect in a safe setting. Many people will go through withdrawal symptoms, developing intense cravings for Internet use as they try to break their addiction. A rehab center provides the structure and support that some people need to get through this challenging part of recovery.

Rehab centers for Internet addiction are modeled on rehab centers for other types of addiction. Many rehab centers provide counseling to help people move forward with their lives in healthy ways. Internet addiction may be masking other emotional and psychological issues. Counselors on-site are able to help people work through those underlying issues in order to reduce the likelihood of relapse. Furthermore, they can help clients learn coping skills that will improve their likelihood of success.

People who go to rehab centers for Internet addiction typically "step down" when they leave. In other words, they do not just leave the center and hope for the best. Instead, they transition to outpatient services, including the help of support groups and individual therapy to aid in the recovery process. The rehab center jump-starts the process, and then the follow-up helps support it over time. This is similar to the way that people leaving drug rehab may go to a sober living house and/or to twelve-step groups to help keep their sobriety. Rehab provides the place to detox from the drug, even when the drug is the Internet.

There are Internet addiction rehab centers all over the world. They are particularly common in Asia, especially in China, Japan, Taiwan, and South Korea. They are also easy to find in Holland and some other areas in Europe. It took the United States a little while to catch up, but these centers are now increasingly available in the United States as well. Some inpatient rehab centers are for all different (or many different) types of addiction including Internet addiction, whereas others are specific to Internet addiction alone. A few of the most well-known Internet addiction treatment centers in the United States include the following:

- reSTART, which is the nation's first recognized Internet addiction treatment center. They offer programs for both teens and adults including step-down programs in later stages of recovery.
- The Computer Addiction Treatment Program, which emphasizes behavioral and cognitive behavioral treatment for Internet addiction including, in particular, gaming addiction.
- Illinois Institute for Addiction Recovery, which is a leader in treating behavioral addictions including Internet addiction. This is a program for adults although they also offer an outpatient program for teens.
- Behavioral Health of the Palm Beaches, Inc., is a Florida-based addiction treatment center that includes treatment for both substances and behavioral addictions including Internet addiction.

Rehab centers are a terrific option for many people. However, they have their drawbacks, the biggest of which is cost. Health insurance may not cover treatment for Internet addiction. Therefore, clients may need to pay out of pocket, and the costs of inpatient care are exorbitant for some families. Plus, of course, the client has to take time off of work or school to attend inpatient care, so it's not always an ideal choice. It's usually reserved for the most severe cases of Internet addiction.

Wilderness Camp/Eco-Therapy

Wilderness camps are another popular option that offer some of the same benefits as rehab centers. These are therapeutic programs that last several days or even several weeks. Participants may live outdoors the entire time (hiking long distances, for example). Alternatively, they may reside in cabins, spending a majority of their days outdoors but off-line.

In either case, wilderness camps offer a disconnection—or detox—from the Internet. Furthermore, they teach survival skills, help people to reconnect with nature, and encourage face-to-face connection with the others in the group. Typically, these camps offer individual and group therapy to help individuals resolve their underlying addiction issues.

There are many good arguments to be made that nature is vital in helping humans heal, particularly those humans who have been out of touch with nature (and themselves) due to Internet addiction. There's a theory called the biophilia hypothesis, which posits that humans have an innate need to seek out nature and other creatures. We need this. And yet, increasingly, we are more and more disconnected from nature. And the more disconnected we become from nature, the more disconnected we become from our inner selves and our fellow humans.

In fact, lack of interaction with nature might cause humans to become both physically and mentally ill, thereby exacerbating the negative effects of Internet addiction. Johann Hari reports on research from the 1970s conducted at the State Prison of Southern Michigan, which found that simply being able to see nature from a cell made prisoners less likely to become ill. Wilderness camps and eco-therapy help to resolve Internet addiction by offering the benefits of nature while also eliminating access to technology.

One example of this form of treatment is the Pacific Quest treatment center, which uses a treatment model that focuses equally on nature, the mind-body connection, and the individual's place within their community. Among other things, they use horticulture therapy to offer sensory integration and somatic experiences that serve as intervention for Internet addiction. They offer services to adolescents and young adults. Outback

Therapeutic Expeditions in Utah and blueFire in Idaho are two more examples of teen wilderness therapy programs for Internet addiction.

Individual Therapy

Of course, not everyone can take the time to enter inpatient treatment in the form of a rehab center or even a wilderness camp. Individual outpatient therapy is another very common treatment option. This is the type of therapy in which you visit a therapist, usually for one hour weekly, to work through your issues. There are many different types of therapists, so it's important to look for one who understands addiction generally and Internet addiction specifically.

Each therapist will approach treatment in their own way. However, this type of therapy commonly incorporates behavior modification, grounding, and mindfulness techniques. Grounding techniques help people to come into the present moment by focusing on their senses. This is particularly important for people with extreme addiction who find themselves dealing with symptoms like psychosis and depersonalization. However, it can be useful for anyone entering therapy to bring them into the room and help them focus on the task at hand.

Likewise, mindfulness practice helps bring people into the present moment. These techniques can be used outside of the therapy room to help work through cravings and sit with uncomfortable feelings instead of turning to the Internet for distraction and numbing. Oftentimes the skills that you learn in the therapy room are what you take with you to actually resolve the issue. Practicing skills of self-control and emotional regulation in therapy will help you deal better with addiction triggers at home.

Behavior modification provides concrete solutions to problems of Internet addiction. For example, a person who always turns on streaming Internet television as soon as they come home from work can learn to instead turn on music. Likewise, someone who immediately picks up their phone when they wake up in the morning can learn to leave it aside and go for a brisk walk before starting their day. Therefore, it's common for Internet addiction therapy to include some form of behavioral therapy such as cognitive behavioral therapy. Therapists may also use other popular interventions and treatment approaches, such as motivational interviewing, which helps the person with addiction gain insight into their problem so that they can work toward change.

In some cases, psychotherapeutic treatment is combined with medication. For example, Kevin Roberts found that many patients see success when they combine naltrexone (a drug that acts on the brain's reward system and is a common treatment for alcoholism) with selective serotonin reuptake inhibitors for depression treatment. It not only treats the depression but also helps treat the addiction. As we learn more and more about the way that Internet use and addiction affect brain chemistry, we'll likely see more and more medication options for treatment.

Family Therapy

Similar to individual therapy, people sometimes also choose couples' counseling or family therapy to help with Internet addiction. Families are systems, and when one part of the system isn't functioning well, it affects the entire system.

Family therapy can help address underlying issues that may be contributing to the addiction. People develop addictions for all different types of reasons. If the family has a history of trauma, then working through the trauma can help alleviate the need to escape that might motivate addictive behavior. If the family has a history of addiction, they can look at that through therapy to help resolve those complex issues and better understand how Internet addiction has become a part of their coping mechanism.

Family therapy for Internet addiction can also help each family member work through pain and problems resulting from the behavior. For example, if parents and teens are fighting over Internet use, then family therapy can help them develop new communication skills and strategies for negotiating Internet time. Parents with concerns about a child's excessive Internet use can learn new ways of talking to their child about the addiction.

Group Therapy

Group therapy is yet another option for people with an Internet addiction. It is often used in combination with individual therapy. For example, a person might see an individual therapist once a week and also attend group therapy once a week. Alternatively, they might see an individual therapist every other week and then have group therapy on the alternate weeks. Of course, sometimes people attend only group therapy and do not choose an individual therapy component at all. Or they may attend individual therapy for a period of time and then switch and attend group therapy (or vice versa). Different approaches work for different people.

Group therapy offers some of the same benefits as both inpatient rehab and outpatient individual therapy. The primary benefit is experiencing the support of other people who are going through the same struggles. Sometimes addiction makes people feel very alone, as though they are the only ones in the world with the problem. When the person with addiction witnesses others going through the same situations, it decreases that sense of isolation and hopelessness. This can be especially important with Internet addiction, since Internet use is a mostly solo activity, despite the illusion of being connected to others. Isolation and loneliness are already a big part of the problem, so reflection back from a group can be an especially powerful part of treatment.

Ironically there are also online support groups for people struggling with Internet addiction. Typically, these are most helpful for people who struggle with a very specific online behavior. In other words, these groups won't help people who are addicted to use in general since the online group is another form of Internet use. However, they can be helpful for people with specific addictions, such as gaming addiction. For example, a woman who lost her son to suicide related to an addiction to the game *EverQuest* launched the support group On-Line Gamers Anonymous (OLGA), which offers daily meetings to support people addicted to gaming as well as to help their loved ones. Kevin Roberts goes far as to argue that "there is something uniquely healing about using the computer and the Internet for recovery as opposed to using them as vehicles for indulging an addiction."

People who are unable or unwilling to access therapy in their communities may find that online therapy or an online support group is a next best option. We'll discuss this further in Chapter 9.

SELF-HELP FOR INTERNET ADDICTION

Internet addiction exists on a spectrum. Some people don't necessarily feel like they need outside help from therapy. However, they do feel like they need to make a shift in their own lives. They want to reduce their Internet usage because they feel like doing so will improve their quality of life. There are many different self-help approaches for people who want to try reducing Internet usage on their own. Note that people in full-blown addiction may not find these solutions helpful enough because they lack external support. One solution for that is to join up with a buddy or find a mentor willing to support you in your efforts, a solution that can be helpful for people in any stage of Internet addiction.

Digital Diet

The digital diet is one of the most popular forms of self-help treatment for Internet addiction. It takes different forms. In fact, there seem to be as many different digital diets as there are different food diets. Some people do technology fasts, others restrict their intake, and still others focus on choosing the "right" usage. In so many ways, the choices mimic popular food diets, including fasting, selecting specific amounts and types of consumption, and focusing on nutrition or wellness rather than just quitting the habit.

Since there are so many different approaches to digital dieting, we won't discuss them all in detail. Generally speaking, a digital diet means that you restrict your intake of Internet media for a period of time, which might be short or could be long. Note that a diet is not typically a lifestyle change. The digital diet is for people who just want a break from their addictive behavior but don't necessarily have any intention of quitting for good.

Here are just a few of the popular approaches to digital dieting:

- Annual Digital Fast, which is comparable to food fasting (similar to the religious fasts of Ramadan, Ash Wednesday, and Yom Kippur). The focus isn't on deprivation but rather the intention to abstain from technology in a meaningful way in order to redirect your attention to spiritual concerns instead of worldly ones.
- "Digital Sabbath," which is a term coined by Anne Dilenschneider for taking a full day each week for nonscreen activities.
- Elimination Diet, in which you stop doing all Internet activities and then slowly add them back one by one to see which ones cause addictive behavior and which don't. You try to cut out the addictive behavior altogether while still enjoying the other activities online.
- No Junk Food, meaning that you only engage in specific, productive online activities such as answering your work email but don't do anything else on the Internet.
- Screen-Free Week, an annual event that actually started as TV Turn-off Week back in 1994 and then became Screen-Free Week in 2010. It's a week-long invitation for schools, families, and organizations to turn off the screens and interact with one another.
- Time-Restriction Diet, which is similar to counting calories in food. You can eat whatever you want but only up to a certain calorie amount, or rather you can consume whatever Internet media you wish but only up to a certain time limit per day or week.

Regardless of the approach, the general idea of a digital diet is to reduce (or eliminate) screen usage, replacing that time with low-tech or analog activities, particularly those that include face-to-face interaction with loved ones and time in nature. Some of the specific features of a digital diet may include the following:

- Choosing to engage with only the most valuable content online
- Downgrading Internet services to just the basics

- Having in-person conversations about each thing you see online to make that content more valuable
- Incorporating tech-free zones into the home or into specific activities such as dining
- Increasing physical activity including using devices while moving instead of sitting
- Only using certain tools, such as Netflix, when you're with other people in order to reduce your tendency to stay home alone and engage with them
- Reducing exposure to all content or to specific content
- Switching to long-form print reading instead of screen reading
- Using only one device at a time (not being on the phone while watching TV)

Of course, we all know that food diets only work temporarily. You eventually give up the diet and go back to your old eating habits. People often find themselves regaining the weight that they lost. Certainly, the same thing can happen with the digital diet. But here's the difference: the digital diet gives your brain a chance to relax and daydream and start working in new ways again. It helps stimulate the neural pathways that you weren't activating when you were constantly online. So, a digital diet may be useful even if you do end up going back to your old ways. And it may also help prevent you from going back to those old ways completely because of the potential to change your brain.

You can also use the diet or food analogy to frame your Internet use in a broader way. Most people agree (even if they don't follow it themselves) that a healthy food diet is one that consists primarily of certain healthy foods while allowing minimal exceptions for junk food. Likewise, a healthy Internet life might consist of engaging mostly in certain activities with limited exceptions for those that pose a higher risk of addiction. In neither case, food or Internet, should you overindulge too often because doing so causes health risks.

Rebooting

Rebooting is another self-help approach, ironically named after the computer itself (powering down for a time). The idea is that you disconnect for a period of time using that time to reconnect with yourself, others, and nature. Then you slowly reintegrate the activities that you want in your online life. This can be similar to a digital diet, particularly the Elimination Diet, but it involves a little bit more of a lifestyle change.

A diet is something that you do, but rebooting is really more about the relationship that you have with yourself as well as with your technology. If you were to reboot, or rekindle, romance with your partner, then it could lead to long-lasting change. That's one of the benefits of the reboot mind-set.

Daniel Sieberg suggests a four-step process for rebooting your relationship with technology:

1. Rethink, during which time you simply notice your Internet usage, assessing it for problem areas and gaining insight into your online experience.
2. Reboot, which is the period of disconnection from all Internet activities.
3. Reconnect, which means that you slowly, steadily, start reintroducing technology in small ways, staying aware of the impact on your mental well-being.
4. Revitalize, which means that you prioritize human connect over Internet usage in an ongoing fashion.

Similarly, Cal Newport offers a two-pronged approach to a digital declutter:

1. Take a break from all optional technologies for one full month. If you have to engage with specific technologies (e.g., work email or texting your child about pickup and drop-off times), then that's okay, but work really hard to eliminate as much as possible for this month-long period. Use the time wisely to (re)discover those analog activities that make your life meaningful.
2. After the month is up, start to slowly and intentionally reintroduce the technologies back into your life. Always ask yourself, "Does bringing this tool back into my life support something that I value deeply?" If it does, then ask yourself, "Is this technology the best way to support that value?" If something offers value and is the best way to get that value, let it back into your life. Otherwise, consider your relationship with it over instead of just rebooted.

Of course, not everyone can completely disconnect from the Internet. Your job may require some online time. However, during that rethinking period, you can become aware of the minimum amount of Internet activity really required as compared to the amount that you do (which is probably far higher). Your reboot might mean disconnecting from all Internet activities except for those that are work related, and you might limit work activities to specific days and times.

Contemplative Computing

Yet another self-help approach is to learn about and incorporate contemplative computing practices. This is a mindfulness approach to technology. Instead of a diet or reboot, it is about learning an entirely new way of life. Of course, it could start with a diet or reboot, and in fact, it almost always starts with some kind of digital elimination. However, the goal is to entirely shift your relationship with technology so that you are using it in the most useful, intentional way possible. This can be the best long-term solution for many people, since we do live in a world that seems to require us to use the Internet on a regular basis.

The term itself—"contemplative computing"—was coined by technology forecaster and author Alex Soojung-Kim Pang, who writes about it extensively in the book *The Distraction Addiction*. He explains that the concept incorporates some of the world's oldest philosophical and religious techniques for managing your "monkey mind" and focusing your attention. However, this is combined with the reality of the twenty-first century and the new scientific information that we have about how humans interact with computers. Our attention and creativity are shaped and influenced by the technology we use; working with that understanding is an important part of contemplative computing.

Pang says that there are four key principles to contemplative computing, each of which is designed to help you redefine your relationship with technology. The first principle is that we can have deep relationships with our technology, to the point where it can actually serve us as an extension of our minds. For example, we no longer need to devote brain space to memorizing people's phone numbers, since our technology does that for us. This isn't a bad thing; it's just a thing, and it can be a good thing if we use it mindfully. The second principle is awareness that the world is increasingly distracting but that there are solutions to that distraction. The third and fourth principles relate to this: we must be contemplative, and in doing so we have the power to redesign the extended mind. In other words, through intentional interaction with our computers, we have the ability to make technology work for us instead of against us.

Contemplative computing starts with something as simple, and ancient, as breathing. And although that may sound ridiculous at first, it's actually surprisingly important. Did you know that there's such a thing as "email apnea"? In sleep apnea, people develop a wide variety of health issues because of the fact that they aren't properly breathing while they sleep. In "email apnea" it's been found that people have a tendency to hold their breath, or breathe more shallowly, as they open email. It has to do with the anticipation of what you're going to find inside the message, and it likely happens as we do all different sorts of online activities. Start paying attention to how much, and how deeply, you do or don't breathe as you engage with your devices.

Of course, "contemplative computing" is just one term (and approach) for a lifestyle technology change. Another example is digital minimalism, which is what Cal Newport had in mind with the digital declutter process described previously. He emphasizes that digital minimalism is "a philosophy of technology." It's not just a series of tips and hacks (although there are approaches that help) but is a way of living. People who embrace minimalism believe that less is more, and you can apply this to your digital life. The goal isn't to eliminate technology but rather to engage with it in the most mindful way possible so that it's always supporting your deepest values and never detracting from the rest of your life. You mindfully choose the Internet activities you want in your life and you optimize them as much as possible. The thirty-day digital declutter can help you break the addiction, but it's the mindful approach to resuming your activity that can help keep you digitally sober in the long term.

Notably, parents can engage in contemplative computing practices, or intentional Internet usage, when designing rules for their children's use. Parents raising children today are raising them with devices, often lots of them starting at a very young age. We know that young brains are at some risk of addiction, but we also don't know the extent of that, and we face the reality that the devices are going to be a part of their daily lives. Therefore, we don't have clear answers about what type of content and for how long each day is good for kids, bad for kids, or neutral. Parents have to make those determinations for themselves. Engaging in mindful practices and paying attention to the effects the experiences have on children, thus implementing some contemplative computer or digital minimalism into their lives, can be one approach. Anya Kamenetz's book *The Art of Screen Time* is one resource for parents interested in learning more about the pros and cons of screens for kids and how to engage mindfully with devices in your own home.

CHAPTER 8

What Is the Underlying Problem?

One of the most controversial aspects of Internet addiction is the fact that it's very hard to differentiate causation from correlation. Causation means that x causes y; for example, that spending too much time on the Internet causes depression. (We don't know that, but that's an example of what would be causation.) Correlation means we can identify that x and y are linked, but we can't say that one causes the other; for example, people who spend more time on the Internet have higher rates of depression, but we can't say for sure that one causes the other. Perhaps having depression makes you more likely to use the Internet, or perhaps there's some other variable that makes both things more likely. When it comes to Internet addiction, there is a lot of difficulty determining cause and effect.

It goes beyond just the chicken-and-egg problem that we've discussed so far. That in and of itself makes understanding Internet addiction a very difficult undertaking. Does the Internet definitely change the brain, or does a preexisting neurological difference make some people's brains more likely to develop an addiction? More than that, though, we simply can't account for all of the different variables that are at play. We can study the brains of children who are engaged with technology, but we can't eliminate all of the other life variables that might be at play in changing their brains.

Life is very different today from two hundred, one hundred, or even twenty years ago. Technology, including the technology at our fingertips daily, plays a huge role in that. But there are many other issues going on for people living in society today. From the chemicals and plastics in the food we eat every day to the regular threats of terrorism and mass shootings, we live with a wide variety of physical and psychological stressors that may differ from those of previous generations. Perhaps the increase in depression is linked more to an increase in awareness, and a decrease in stigma, that allows for more frequent identification. In other words, maybe people aren't more depressed; maybe they're just reporting it more and dealing with it more publicly. We don't know. There are a lot of factors.

Even if we limit the conversation just to the problems of smartphones, can we say with 100 percent certainty that what's changing our brains is the actual tactile individual use of these objects, or could it be a completely different effect, caused by the electromagnetic energy pulsating in the air all around us? Our brains are electric, after all, and surely that electricity in the air must have some impact on them. Maybe people have more headaches not because of eye strain from facing those screens all day but because of electromagnetic sensitivity. Maybe people's attention spans are shrinking because of factors that have little or nothing to do with physically being on our devices so often. So even if we blame the phone, it might not be the act of engaging in behavioral addiction causing all of our physical and mental health issues. Or it might be. The fact is, we don't really know.

Of course, legitimate scientific studies do all that they can to account for all of those other variables. Cal Newport summarizes how psychology professor and author Jean Twenge found that people born after 1995 had significantly higher rates of anxiety, depression, and suicide. She compared data going back decades (in some cases as far back as 1930), and she accounted for myriad variables "from stressful current events to increased academic pressure" but found that despite deep investigation into other causes, the only seeming difference between this generation and the others was the existence, availability, and use of smartphones and social media. This is one example of how established researchers have done deep dives into other possible explanations and continued to find enough support to believe that even though there are other factors at play, the prevalent use of the Internet is responsible for some serious problems facing individuals in our society today, problems that may lead to widespread addiction.

We can see that there are changes in individuals and in society over time. Studies show that there's a correlation with increased Internet usage. There might even be a case for causation. However, we're just beginning to understand the impact of the Internet, let alone Internet addiction, so it's challenging to say for sure exactly what the ramifications are. We can make very educated guesses, and we can keep researching; keeping the conversation open and ongoing can help us learn more about the issue.

As we research Internet addiction, we have to face the fact that we can't say for sure that the widespread problems in our society are directly linked with increased Internet usage, although they likely do have some link. That's at the macro level. But what about the micro level? In other words, let's look at any one individual who develops an Internet addiction. Can we say for sure that the addiction causes the problems (or vice versa, that specific things put that person at risk and caused the addiction)? Or are we unable to parse that out? For example, if a person with an Internet addiction also has social anxiety, can their doctor say for sure that the Internet addiction caused the social anxiety or, conversely, that the social anxiety made them turn to the Internet, and then they became addicted?

As with all types of addiction, the truth is probably somewhat murkier than one or the other. Let's consider substance addiction, to a very commonly used (and perhaps misused) drug: caffeine. Imagine that you've had a very restless night. You couldn't sleep, you tossed and turned, and when you finally started to dream, the alarm went off. Groggily, you snoozed a few times, but you needed to get up and get going because you had to be at work. With glazed eyes and a slight headache, you reached immediately for a cup of hot coffee. As the coffee kicked in, your headache subsided, the sleepiness went away, and you embarked on your day. During the commute, you were irritable with the other passengers. Maybe this is so normal that you didn't even notice how grumpy you felt. But if you noticed, could you say for sure why? Were you irritable because you were still tired, because you weren't feeling great, because the caffeine was kicking in and starting to make you restless, because you hadn't eaten, or because of some other factor we haven't even considered? If you'd had three cups of coffee instead of one, would you have felt differently? Once we look at something as seemingly innocuous as coffee, we realize just how hard it is to define addiction and how much harder it is to separate cause and effect.

Consider, first: is this really an addiction to coffee? Arguably, even if you insist on having your daily coffee, find it hard to stop even if you want to, and develop withdrawal symptoms (like headaches) when you don't have it, it's still not an addiction if it's not causing problems in your work, in your financial and social life, or to your health. Most daily coffee drinkers do not consider it to be a problem and wouldn't consider it an addiction. Plenty of reports indicate that it might even be healthy to have coffee every day. But is it affecting your sleep? Maybe the reason you tossed and turned the night before was because you had too much caffeine in your system that day. Is it affecting your relationships if you're so irritable every morning? These are subtle things. They certainly don't rise to the level of harm that we see in most types of drug addiction. But it goes to highlight that it's hard to define what an addiction is.

And it's even tougher to determine cause and effect. Were you tired because your system was already off from caffeine the day before, or did you need caffeine because you were tired? Were you grumpy because the caffeine hadn't kicked in or because it had or because of some unrelated issue? What was the cause and effect? If you removed the drug entirely, would there still be a problem? And that's where we can get back to the Internet. If someone has an Internet addiction, and you remove all access to the Internet (which, of course, is a challenge in and of itself in today's society), would there still be a problem? Would society as a whole still have these huge sweeping issues of decreased empathy and increased attention deficits? Would the individual still have those problems, or would they resolve themselves? If the Internet addict had never been exposed to the Internet, would there still be an issue? Does it matter, given that the Internet is a reality of today's world and there aren't going to be many people who have never been exposed to it?

We know two things for sure: addictions existed long before the Internet and so did most, if not all, of the problematic symptoms that we associated with Internet addiction. So, the person with an addiction to Internet pornography may be a twenty-first-century character, but people have been addicted to pornography since long before the Internet existed. The person with a pornography addiction may have similar symptoms of depression and feeling numb to interaction with real live humans, whether that addiction is to Internet porn or old-fashioned erotic literature.

The argument on one hand is that these problems have always existed and that the Internet is just one more way to facilitate them. The argument on the other hand is that the speed and expanse of the Internet has exacerbated those existing problems, perhaps creating a new level of addiction if not an entirely new type of addiction.

Consider this: in her book about the benefits of reading aloud, author Meghan Cox Gurdon reports on fascinating research from Dr. John Hutton at Cincinnati Children's Hospital working to understand how young children's brains react differently to hearing a story read aloud with no visuals as compared to with still images (e.g., those in a print book) and animated images (e.g., those on a screen). What they found was that in very young children's brains, there were five key areas that were most engaged when they heard a story read aloud and looked at still images—this perfect combination of auditory and visual stimulation along with the need to employ some imagination had the best effect in growing children's neural networks. The different parts of the brain all linked together. In comparison, when just hearing a story with no visual images at all, the young children had to work too hard to come up with their own meanings, so while some parts of the brain were well stimulated, others were not. This applies specifically to young children who haven't necessarily developed a strong bank of images for their imagination yet.

So, what does that have to do with Internet addiction? That's where the third scenario becomes very important: what happens to children's brains when they hear a story while also watching animation, as they do on a screen? Their brains stop engaging almost at all. The visual part of the brain is highly stimulated, but it seems completely separated from the rest of the brain. As the children watch the animation, they stop employing any sort of curiosity or imagination. The higher-order parts of the brain just turn off. The brain works better just hearing a story and not seeing anything at all than it does when hearing a story combined with viewing animated images. Watching those images turns the rest of the brain off.

Obviously, this has huge implications for the dangers of screen time for young children. Gurdon makes a great case for replacing, or at least supplementing, young children's screen time with reading aloud with kids. But this also has important implications for Internet addiction for people of any age. It highlights the fact that our brains act differently when engaging with screen technology than they do with other types of media. Can you become addicted to reading books? Sure, possibly; they're a great escape, but you aren't going to develop the same kind of addiction to them as you are to online reading with all of its hyperlinked text, moving animation, and other forms of distraction.

If we completely removed the Internet from our society, there would be people who got addicted to the same types of content that addicts them online. But it wouldn't be as easy. The addiction might not go so deep. And there would likely be mitigating factors that would help keep that addiction in check. People had shopping addictions years ago, but they had to physically go to the store, spend their cash, and face the cashiers (who often knew them and their families personally). This not only meant natural restrictions on the behavior itself (after all, who wants to hit the same store three times in a week when that judgmental clerk is going to be there again?) but also incorporated some protective factors. For example, if you were shopping because you were depressed or lonely, going out to engage with the world was part of what helped.

Then came the Home Shopping Network and catalogs and the ability to order anything you wanted on the phone. It became easier to engage in addictive shopping behavior, because the clerk on the other end of the phone was anonymous and you were anonymous to them. Plus, you didn't have to leave the house. You could impulsively shop more easily because there were less barriers to making your purchases. And there were less protections; you weren't engaging directly face-to-face with people any-more to help soothe the underlying issues that made you want to shop. And today, of course, we can easily shop online at any minute of any day without ever engaging in even voice contact with another human being. We can get same-day delivery and, in some instances, don't even need to be home to deal with the other human delivering the package. If we sud-denly removed online shopping from our society, some people would still have a shopping addiction and new people would still develop it, but it wouldn't happen as easily and therefore would likely be less prevalent. Some of the people who have that addiction might venture out into the face-to-face world to do their shopping and discover that some of those protective benefits of doing so help reduce the addiction itself.

Someone who is prone to addiction in general—because of brain chem-istry, life circumstances, or (most likely) the intersection of both—can develop addiction anyway, regardless of access to the Internet. But the Internet sure makes it easier to develop the addiction and perhaps harder to break it. So maybe we can't say which came first—the problem we're masking with addiction or the addiction itself—but we can say with fairly strong certainty that the Internet complicates things. It likely makes addic-tion more prevalent in our society. This correlates with other widespread issues in our society including serious mental health issues. And the indi-vidual who has an Internet addiction may benefit from learning which issue came first, but they don't necessarily need to know that in order to start addressing their own problems.

COMORBIDITY/DUAL DIAGNOSIS

Many of the problematic effects of Internet addiction are mental health issues. Just like at the societal level, it's hard to say at the individual level which problem came first. Did your teen develop depression because they were on the Internet too much? Or did they increasingly turn to the Inter-net because they already had symptoms of depression that they were trying to self-medicate? Does it matter? Even if we can't tell the cause and the effect, we can talk about comorbidity and dual diagnosis. In other words, we can acknowledge that both things exist for the individual as serious, likely related, problems. The teen has depression and Internet addiction, and it doesn't necessarily matter if one causes the other because you can treat them both as serious mental health issues, ones that likely reinforce each other, and each requiring attention and treatment.

When I first started writing this chapter, I realized that I wasn't certain that I knew the difference between comorbidity and dual diagnosis. This surprised me. I have a master's degree in psychological studies. I read psychology literature regularly. This is a very basic topic of addiction. How could I not know the difference? But then I started digging in, and I realized that it's because there's a lot of really confusing, conflicting usage of the two terms (and incidentally, a third term, "co-occurring disorders"). Before I digress for a second, let me clarify that what we're basically talking about here is the existence of two different diagnosable issues in one person—such as when someone has a diagnosis for both Internet addiction and anxiety. We're about to read some conflicting definitions (I promise, the reason for even getting into this will reveal itself shortly), so just keep in the back of your mind that more or less, despite these differences, we mean two separate mental health issues in one person.

Now, for the digression. Some legitimate, well-recognized sources say that there is absolutely no difference between these terms. Others say that there's a subtle difference between comorbidity and dual diagnosis. But they seem to disagree vastly on the difference. For example, some sources say that dual diagnosis refers only to times when a person is diagnosed with both an addiction and a psychiatric illness, whereas others say that a dual diagnosis can be any two diagnosed issues at the same time including physical health issues. So, by those latter standards, someone with both diabetes and depression would have a dual diagnosis, but that same person would not have a dual diagnosis by the first definition.

The confusion deepens when you try to not just understand the nuances of dual diagnosis but also separate it out from comorbidity. Let's go with the first definition of dual diagnosis given previously: when a person is diagnosed with both an addiction and a psychiatric illness. Some sources say that comorbidity is the exact same thing as that. Others say comorbidity is when a person has both an addiction and a mental health diagnosis but not necessarily at the same time; in other words, someone has an addiction and then resolves it but later develops depression. Still others say that comorbidity means that the person has both an addiction and a mental health issue at the same time but more specifically that the mental health issue is directly linked to the addiction (either causing it or worsened by it).

It took me a little while to parse this out. I dug deeper and deeper to find increasingly legitimate sources for definitions. And then I realized something interesting. Although certainly individual people have had two or more diagnoses at the same time for years upon years, the term "dual diagnosis" is relatively new. It was really only in the late 1980s that people started using the term, and they also used the term "co-occurring disorders" at that time. It was also then that researchers began in-depth study into the relationship between mental health and addiction. They weren't any exact terms in use as the research developed. It's not as though there's a specific regulating body that says, "We're going to use this term, only this term, and only to mean this." So different researchers were using different terminologies to mean similar things. And we have to consider that this happened only within the past few decades, which is right around the time we started using the Internet. Just when a lot of the research into dual diagnosis was becoming mainstream, so were computers in the home. As the years went on, the research continued, and so did ever-increasing use of the Internet to access and spread information. So, it's little wonder that we don't have a clear-cut definition of comorbidity versus dual diagnosis; there are many different (legitimate and less so) researchers and reporters spreading those words around without ever agreeing on a definition. The Internet itself complicates the matter of agreeing on definitions about problems associated with the Internet.

So, that was the digression into why the terms aren't so clear-cut and why that matters. But now we'll get back to the meat of the matter, which is that it is very common for someone with an Internet addiction to also have one or more other mental health issues. As we saw earlier in this book, depression and anxiety are particularly prevalent among people with Internet addiction. We could debate endlessly which one caused, or exacerbated, the other, but when it comes to treatment, it's not all that important. What's important is that the individual has two (or more) serious issues that rise to the level of a diagnosis and therefore require intervention and treatment. If your child has violent aggressive outbursts when their phone is taken away and also has such terrible social anxiety that they've stopped going to school, it doesn't really matter much whether the phone addiction caused the anxiety or the anxiety caused them to cling to the phone; what matters is that they have both issues and you must treat them both as serious.

One of the problems that arise, though, is the complexity of trying to treat someone with a dual diagnosis. (Note that for the rest of this book, we're going to use the terms "dual diagnosis," "comorbidity," and "co-occurring disorders" interchangeably to refer to someone who has both an addiction—specifically an Internet addiction since that's the topic of this book—and another mental health diagnosis.) As we saw in the previous chapter, there are many different treatment options for Internet addiction. Naturally, there are also many different treatment options for each second mental health diagnosis. And so, of course, there are going to be many different ways of approaching treatment for someone who has co-occurring disorders.

The best treatment option for dual diagnosis clients is something that the addiction community has been debating since the community first started using the term. Generally speaking, you can either treat one problem first or treat both problems simultaneously. For example, if someone has both addiction and depression, you might first treat the addiction and then deal with the depression. Alternatively, the individual may work simultaneously with multiple professionals to treat both the addiction and the depression at the same time. There are good arguments to be made for either approach. What works best for one individual may not work well for another.

Consider, for example, someone who is so far immersed in active addiction that all they can think about is their next fix. Every single thing that they do all day long is geared toward getting that fix. They also have a history of an eating disorder. But the doctor can't tell right now if they're not eating because of the eating disorder or if they're not eating because their priority is getting the drug. In such a case, it might make sense to treat the addiction first, in order to alleviate the symptoms related to just that issue so as to make the best determination about what treatment, if any, is necessary to help with the eating disorder. Removing the complicating factors of the addiction helps the doctor better see what the real issue is as far as the eating disorder. On the other hand, if the person's eating disorder is so bad that they are on the verge of death because of lack of nutrients, then it would make sense to treat both issues at the same time, encouraging healthier eating habits while also dealing with the addiction.

People with a dual diagnosis who go to inpatient rehab often deal with both issues simultaneously, although there may first be a short period of detox that focuses on getting the person unhooked from their addictive substance. People who go to outpatient therapy may first deal with their addiction and then their other issue or may deal with both at the same time, depending greatly on which professionals they're working with, what they've told those professionals, and how serious each of the issues is.

Treatment may also change over time as one or both of the conditions start to resolve. For example, think about someone who has both an Internet addiction and an anxiety disorder. Working to quit the addictive behavior may temporarily cause the person to be even more anxious than usual. In the long term, the Internet use may be making the anxiety worse, but in the immediate moment, it can feel like it helps reduce anxiety. Trying to quit, and going through withdrawal, may worsen the anxiety in the moment, even though quitting in the long term could help resolve anxiety issues. Therefore, in the short term, when withdrawal symptoms from the

Internet are at their worst and anxiety is at its peak, the individual may benefit from antianxiety medications. They take the medication to deal with the anxiety while working through the Internet addiction. When the addiction is resolved, they may choose to address their anxiety in new ways, such as through cognitive behavioral therapy, and opt to wean off their medication. They may, or may not, find that this causes a relapse in Internet addiction. When dealing with a dual diagnosis, treatment is complicated, but it isn't impossible.

In fact, treating one issue often goes a long way toward helping resolve the other. For example, someone who treats their Internet addiction with wilderness therapy may find that the treatment helps reduce their symptoms of depression. Maybe getting off of the Internet helps, maybe it's being in nature, maybe it's being with all of the people in the group, and likely it's a combination of all of these things. In any case, even if the depression existed prior to the Internet addiction, treating the addiction may help treat the depression. The most important thing with dual diagnosis is recognizing both issues as serious and working with professionals who understand both conditions.

People can have a dual diagnosis of Internet addiction and just about any other mental health issue. Anyone with a mental health issue could potentially develop an Internet addiction. Each individual is unique, and what they may or may not fall prey to is unique. That said, research indicates that anxiety and depression are the two most common types of disorders that are dual-diagnosed with Internet addiction. Of course, they're also the two most common disorders diagnosed in general, so it makes sense that their numbers are also high for dual diagnosis. Studies indicate that there's also a correlation, and a high likelihood of dual diagnosis, for people with Internet addiction and the following issues:

- Aggression disorders including conduct disorder and oppositional-defiant disorder
- All mood disorders, not just limited to major depression
- Attention deficit hyperactivity disorder (ADHD) including adult-onset ADHD
- Personality disorders, such as borderline personality disorder and schizoid personality disorder, although further research is necessary in this area
- Schizophrenia and/or dissociative conditions
- Sleep disorders, as discussed previously in this book
- Specific forms of anxiety including social phobia and obsessive compulsive disorder

People with an Internet addiction are also more likely to receive a diagnosis of another substance use disorder. They are more likely to develop addiction to nicotine and alcohol, as well as to other substances. A 2010 study by Case Western Reserve University School of Medicine found that teens sending more than 120 texts per day were twice as likely to have tried drinking and 40 percent more likely to have used illegal drugs. Teens engaging in three or more hours of social media per day were 84 percent more likely to have used illegal drugs.

There is some debate about whether or not having an Internet addiction and a substance addiction is truly dual diagnosis. If Internet addiction looks the same in the brain as cocaine addiction, then does a person addicted to both the Internet and cocaine have one diagnosis or two? Regardless of which side of that debate you land on, the research indicates that Internet addiction correlates with higher likelihood of other addictions.

Of course, if you have one type of Internet addiction, you're also more likely to develop a second type. For example, if you have an addiction to surfing the web generally, you might also develop a specific addiction to a particular type of content such as online auctions or catfishing. If you have a gaming addiction, then you're more likely than someone who doesn't to develop an addiction to social media or Internet pornography. In fact, Kevin Roberts reports that 90 percent of the people who come to him and receive a diagnosis of online gaming addiction also have a second diagnosis, most commonly autism spectrum disorders, ADHD, or depression.

The more time that you spend online, the more likely you are to engage in more than one addictive behavior online. That's not a dual diagnosis, per se, but it's worth being aware of. If you have a gaming addiction, don't think that you're safe just because you stop gaming; you likely have to monitor all of your other online uses as well. When reSTART launched as a treatment center for Internet addiction, it attempted to include both women and men in the program together. However, they quickly found that people in recovery for Internet addiction were at great risk of developing sex addiction, made more problematic by coed programs.

This brings us to one final aspect of this exploration into the underlying problem of Internet addiction, which is the question of whether this addiction might sometimes be used as a "healthier" addiction to replace something that's more damaging. If someone has a drug addiction that's ruining their lives because of the financial and legal consequences of that addiction, and they replace that addiction with an Internet addiction, then is the Internet addiction truly a problem? The underlying issue, whatever is causing the tendency to addiction in the first place, might still be there. But if the person's Internet addiction is comparatively harmless, then is it really so bad? Of course, in order to qualify as an addiction, it has to do some harm to the individual. But if their work performance suffers slightly, yet is so much better than it was when the person had a drug addiction, then is it truly a problem?

The answer is highly individual. It goes back to the concept of harm reduction. Someone who has another addiction, including one to substances, is more at risk of developing an Internet addiction. People who are in recovery may find themselves staying away from their usual drug of choice and turning to the Internet instead. Complete abstinence from all addictive substances and behaviors may be ideal, but it may not be possible. Some people might argue that for them it's not even ideal. They don't mind having an addiction; they just want to mitigate the harm. If so, then turning to the Internet, even if that behavior becomes addictive, might not be so bad. But do consider the risks. Someone with an addiction who replaces their substance with the Internet but doesn't resolve the underlying issues related to addiction more generally may find themselves slipping further and further into their new addiction. It may become more harmful. It may lead to a relapse of the initial drug of choice. It may even become a channel to access that drug, through addiction to the Dark Net, for example. So, on the one hand, harm reduction certainly says that the Internet addiction may be healthier than the substance addiction, but it still recognizes that there are potential risks involved. The individual should be aware of those risks as they work toward recovery and mitigating harm. Once again, it doesn't really matter if the drug addiction or the Internet addiction came first if one or both of them start to ruin your life.

We saw early on in this book that there are many ways to define Internet addiction. We've worked out a basic definition that clinicians can use or that we can look at to self-diagnose if there's a problem. More or less, that works. However, it's worth noting that one of the major reasons that it's difficult to diagnose an Internet addiction is because we as a society have no scale for what "normal" use might be. If we can't figure out what's relatively normal or "okay," then we can't easily discern what's abnormal or troubling. Is it normal or okay to spend an hour per day on social media? What about five hours? The technology is so insidious and the changes are happening so rapidly that we as a society haven't figured out what's normal. Do you think it would be normal for a person to lose eleven years of their life to handheld devices alone, not even including their computers, televisions, and gaming consoles? That probably (hopefully) doesn't sound normal to you, and yet, Meghan Cox Gurdon cites research from technology writer Adam Alter that shows that based on current average usage rates, that's exactly what the average, "normal" person is doing.

They're spending eleven years on their cell phones and tablets, years that could be spent on something else. Is that addiction?

Are we all becoming a little bit addicted? In his book *iDisorder*, Larry Rosen makes a detailed argument about how the average person in society is manifesting many of the symptoms of various mental health issues as a direct result of the relationship they have with their phone. In other words, even if your Internet use doesn't rise to the level of addiction, and even if you don't meet all the criteria of a second diagnosis, you may find that increasing Internet use has caused you to develop many of the symptoms of a second diagnosis, such as depression or a personality disorder. For example, you might not be truly addicted to the Internet or have a narcissistic personality, but with increasing Internet use, you may develop some of the less-than-pleasant symptoms of narcissism. One of the symptoms is lack of empathy; the more you use Tinder for instant gratification hookups or tweet angry, thoughtless responses to people's comments, the more you may start to exhibit signs of lacking empathy. Are you diagnosable? No. But is it of concern? Perhaps.

CHAPTER 9

But Aren't There Benefits to the Internet?

This is a book about Internet addiction. It's about the most problematic uses of the technology we love today. It's about the worst-case scenarios. Naturally, it's focused on the negatives. But I hope that hasn't given you the impression that I hate technology or I am opposed to it. I'm not. I love technology. Throughout the year or more that I researched and worked on this book, I read a lot of terrifying information that suggests that all of us are becoming increasingly addicted to our devices, and I certainly questioned my own use regularly, but I didn't give up my own phone during that time. I curtailed use here and there, trying to implement some contemplative computing practices into my own life, as well as to look experientially at what level of addiction I might have myself. However, I didn't quit social media or even give up my phone for a full day. While we could debate back and forth about whether or not that choice has to do with my own potential Internet addiction, the point is that I'm personally happy to have a cell phone and to spend time on it. I'm not the only one.

Very few people in our society, even those who recognize the widespread and growing problem of Internet addiction, suggest a return to a pre-Internet society. First of all, the train has already left the station. We aren't going backward, and most likely the Internet and the similar technologies that will follow it in the future are here to stay. So, it's pointless to talk about getting rid of it altogether. But more than that, there are some really awesome, wonderful things about the Internet that have made our society better. We wouldn't even know about the effect of technology (or drugs, or anything else) on the brain if we didn't have the computer technology to do that research. And more and more of us can access and understand that information thanks to the Internet.

There are people who land on either extreme end of the pros versus cons of technology argument. Some people believe that social media, or the Internet more generally, is leading to the end of the world, the downfall of humankind, and the destruction of all good things on our planet. Other people believe that technology itself can solve anything, that it's perfectly fine that our brains are changing because that's just what happens with evolution, and that the world is always better off when we're connected to the Internet. Most of us, however, land somewhere in the middle. We like the Internet and don't intend to give it up, recognizing the many benefits that it offers, but we also have a creeping feeling in our guts that we could be better using some of those online hours engaged in more socially proactive, concretely creative behavior.

It's important to understand that this type of debate has taken place with every single big technological change in our society. In fact, even though today we all generally agree that long-form book reading has terrific benefits for almost everyone, there was a lot of controversy about the potential harms of books. Back when words first began being put to paper, there were many critics who said that this would harm oral history and prevent people from utilizing their memories in the future. In the nineteenth century, a librarian named Mary A. Bean made a big fuss about the damage reading could do to children because the content in some books could damage young minds. In the 1960s, some librarians were opposed to the fact that libraries were beginning to offer multimedia materials like filmstrips and tape recordings because this was unreliable or fragmented information. And books aren't the only tools that have had their critics. From clocks to electric lights, people have always been concerned when new technology becomes ubiquitous. The Internet is just another extension of this. One could argue that this means all of the fear around addiction to it is unnecessary hype. Alternatively, one could argue that we've been progressively changing our society and our brains with technology and that this is one step further in a continuous problem.

There's a lot to debate there, but this isn't the place for it. Let's assume that we are all likely to keep using the Internet to some degree. It brings a lot of benefits to us individually and collectively. We also recognize that for some people it can become an addiction, and that can be a huge problem. Within that context, let's talk about the times and ways in which the benefits of the Internet balance out or even outweigh the problems associated with addiction to it. To do that, we need to look specifically at the mental health benefits of Internet usage.

Benefits of the Internet for Autism Spectrum Disorders

Let's start by going back to a topic that we already touched on briefly: the use of the Internet by people on the autism spectrum, particularly those who have nonverbal autism. Technology has the potential to offer people with this disorder the ability to communicate with others around them. This opens up a whole new world, not just online, but in their everyday relationships.

Meghan Cox Gurdon offers a great example of this in her book, sharing the story of an autistic boy named Gabe. His parents had tried reading aloud to him when he was young but mistakenly believed that he didn't enjoy the experience, so they stopped doing so. Over the years he became, in his own words, addicted to screens. A professional in his life recognized the potential in that and introduced a type of screen interaction that would allow Gabe to begin communicating with his parents through the technology. They discovered that they had misunderstood his cues for all of those years and that he was actually enjoying interaction with them much more than they had thought. They began to read aloud to him again. He is quoted as saying that although he is addicted to screens, he would rather hear someone read aloud to him all day every day if that were possible than be on the devices. The technology facilitated his ability to communicate the ways in which his family could better connect with him. If it weren't for the screens, they might never have learned that, so even if it's true that he is "addicted" to screen technology (his own word), for that family, the benefits outweighed the harms.

People on the autism spectrum, whether verbal or not, have trouble with communication. They may not pick up on social cues, and this can cause a lot of awkward, uncomfortable interaction. Research suggests that social media can provide a helpful medium for practicing communication. In fact, a 2017 study completed at Yale University found that teens with ASD reported better quality friendships when they utilized social media to aid in communication. The study further found that although teens with ASD did experience some level of anxiety related to that online communication, the benefits of communicating with others via social media outweighed the drawbacks of the anxiety.

The same was not true for teens without ASD, suggesting that there's a particular benefit to this medium for people with autism. Perhaps the medium of social media levels the playing field a little bit. In-person communication requires reading a lot of nonverbal cues, trying to understand subtleties in voice and inflection so as to pick up on sarcasm, irony, and so forth. There simply aren't as many of those cues online. Therefore, all people online are navigating the tricky world of trying to understand one another without those cues. For people without autism, that's a drawback; it's often what leads to miscommunication online that can result in breakups, arguments, and so forth. However, for people with ASD who already experience that disadvantage in communication, it's just par for the course. If people with ASD, particularly children and teens, can work with others such as parents and counselors to discuss those nuances, then online communication can enhance their relationships. If a teen on the spectrum uses social media to connect with friends and also has conversations with parents who help them to understand what a particular online interaction might mean from the other person's point of view, then they get the benefit of learning more about communication while on that even playing field with the other person.

Social media, texting, and other online communication also give the person with ASD the opportunity to take the time that they need to respond. Although these mediums feel very immediate, they do allow for a pause in the way that in-person conversations sometimes lack. Particularly in groups, people with ASD may find themselves standing on the sidelines as the conversation flies back and forth, whereas online they can interject more easily when they are ready to do so. Being able to communicate with the same people both online and in person gives those people the chance to better understand the person with ASD, making them more likely to engage positively with them when they're in the real world.

The benefits don't just apply to teens with ASD. Adults on the spectrum also seem to benefit from moderate social media use. One study published in the journal *Cyberpsychology, Behavior, and Social Networking* found that adults with ASD who used Facebook in moderation were happier than those who did not. Notably, they didn't find a happiness increase when those same adults used Twitter, so more research is necessary to determine the subtleties of when and how social media can help people with ASD, but signs do indicate that there are a lot of potential positives.

The Internet is also the perfect place for people with autism to explore their special interests. We saw in an earlier chapter how that can become problematic when it leads to addiction that feels destructive to the person. However, it can also be a positive. The individual gets very passionate about their special interests, but the people in their own lives may not have the patience or willingness to continuously listen to in-depth information about obscure topics. Even the well-intentioned neurotypical parent or friend may get tired of listening to the intricate details of different types of trains or the eating habits of dinosaurs. The Internet provides an opportunity to meet other people who are also deeply interested in these particular topics.

Special interests are not just a minor hobby to the person with ASD. They can be a way that the person self-soothes, keeping them functioning in their lives particularly during times of high stress. The individual may find that exploring their special interests helps them feel grounded, restores energy, and improves their ability to handle challenging situations. Of course, the individual can explore a special interest on their own. They can use the Internet to do so. But connecting with others in a social way to share that special interest can provide a particularly positive level of relational interaction that adds additional mental health benefits. The Internet provides a place to make such connections.

Finding people who share the same interests, or the same struggles, as you do is one of the key benefits of the Internet. Research indicates that families with children on the autism spectrum benefit from this in that they can use the Internet to connect to the autism community. People in their everyday lives might not understand all that they are going through and therefore aren't always able to offer enough support, understanding, or advice. Going online to connect with others through social media allows parents and other family members to get that support. Support for caregivers in not to be underestimated. Caregivers of all kinds (not just those dealing with ASD issues) suffer a lot of stress and can end up in poor mental health as a result. Finding communities to help them can be hugely protective. Increasingly, those communities are accessible online.

BENEFITS FOR PEOPLE WHO FEEL ISOLATED

When I did an informal poll of the people I'm connected to online, the vast majority said that the reason that they love social media is because it allows them to feel connected to others who are similar to them. Finding the communities that can support you offers huge benefits, no matter who you are and what you are struggling with. People feel isolated or "different" for a vast array of different reasons. Being able to go online to connect with others who understand them, express similar views, and offer support can be hugely beneficial. It can't replace in-person connection, and the risk of addiction can lead people to use it as a replacement in a way that's harmful, but it's also better than nothing, so the person who doesn't feel like they can connect with others in real life is better off connecting online than not connecting at all.

There are many people who are limited in their real-life connections because they are housebound or have limited social activity due to mental and/or physical health issues. If you literally can't leave your house because you are physically unable to do so, then having an online community can serve as a lifeline to protect your mental health. Likewise, if you have limited access to a diverse community of people who understand you (e.g., you live in a very small, isolated town), then finding people who do respect and empathize with you can be a lifesaver, despite the fact that those people may "only" exist online.

Back in 2012, I authored a book called *Crochet Saved My Life*, in which I interviewed about two dozen women about the health benefits of crafting. One of those women, Marinke, expressed that crochet had helped her as she coped with depression and social anxiety related in part to her experiences as someone on the autism spectrum. Over the next few years, she connected with a large number of people online, sharing the beauty of the craft of crochet. She began to design crochet patterns, particularly colorful mandalas, and she even published a book of her work. Sadly, after a few years of doing well, depression came back, and she died by suicide. When that happened, I felt real, strong grief despite the fact that I "only" knew her through online communication. I launched a project in her honor, Mandalas for Marinke, through which hundreds of people contributed crocheted mandalas, mostly using Marinke's designs, to raise awareness about depression and suicide. Many, many of those people expressed how deeply affected they were by her death. They didn't know her "in person," but she had played a very real role in their lives, blogging and using social media to share not just her love of crafting but also her challenges with mental health. In this instance, many people felt real grief, which is, of course, the risk that you take when engaging in serious relationships. The community also came together online to honor her and support each other through that grief. This is just one example out of so many showing how the relationships that people form online are genuine, authentic, and deep. For all the shallow interactions that form the negative side of online life, there are also these very meaningful relationships. For anyone suffering from social isolation for any reason at all, those relationships can't be underestimated.

People can feel isolated because they are literally housebound. They may feel isolated because a mental health disorder, including ASD, separates them from others due to communication problems, differences in understanding one another, and so forth. Or they may be different in a way that causes people in the real world to bully and judge them—someone who is very overweight, someone who is transgendered, someone who is "different" and unfortunately lives in a place where difference is not accepted. Any of these things can drastically impact the person's mental well-being, and the Internet has the potential to provide a safe space for that person to get through those challenges. It's not always a safe space, as we've seen. And even when it is, there's the risk of becoming so comfortable in that space that the individual opts out of the real world, limiting themselves in ways that are unhealthy. It's not either-or; the Internet has risks but can also provide massive benefits particularly for people who are suffering in real life. That benefit is not to be underestimated even as we consider the risks. This potential to go either way is what makes understanding Internet addiction such a complex issue.

BENEFITS OF ONLINE GAMING

As we discussed previously, one of the most-studied forms of Internet addiction is addiction to online gaming. It comes with a lot of risks. But it, too, has another side. There are benefits, including social benefits and mental health benefits, to online gaming. Even though it poses such a great risk of Internet addiction, it's not all bad and may at times be a good thing.

Massively multiplayer online role-playing games (MMORPGs), such as *World of Warcraft*, have the most potential for addiction. But they also have the ability to teach players important life skills and give them the opportunity to practice them. Those skills include working together with others as a team; planning ahead and adapting to changes in a narrative or situation; engaging in real-time communication (which is often voice communication); improving skills in reading, problem-solving, and math; and developing fine motor skills as well as hand-eye coordination.

Research published in the January 2014 issue of *American Psychologist* found overwhelming potential benefit in four key areas of life: cognitive, motivational, emotional, and social. They emphasize that many of the key benefits of gaming for children in particular come from the fact that gaming is a type of play and that children engage in play to work through many of their emotional challenges in life. When children go to therapy, for example, they don't sit and talk to a therapist like an adult might. Instead, they play games, which is how they express themselves and problem solve, especially when they don't have the words to explain what they're going through. While there are certainly differences between online gaming and playing tag or soccer with your real-life friends, the authors of this research argue that many of the benefits of play can be found in online game play just like they are in real life.

In addition to the benefits of play, they found that gaming offers other widespread benefits. For example, they found that people who play shooter games have improved attention allocation as well as better spatial skills. This may correlate with long-term success in science, math, and technology. Notably, they agree that Internet use and gaming change the brain, which is one of the biggest issues in addiction, but they argue that those brain changes aren't necessarily a bad thing. These games may change the brain in ways that improve performance and ability over time. That said, they noted that different games have different benefits; games that weren't shooter games didn't change the brain in these same potentially beneficial ways.

Another benefit of some games is a self-esteem boost that they offer. MMORPG, in particular, may offer self-esteem benefits for some players. Games are set up to offer continuous rewards. The addictive side of that is the dopamine hit it gives, but it also provides positive reinforcement, which can help boost feelings of good self-esteem. This is magnified when team members also provide positive reinforcement. Setting and meeting goals in a game can make the player feel more competent. Getting peer support enhances that. Since negative self-esteem correlates with many mental health problems, including but certainly not limited to eating disorders, activities that boost self-esteem can be an important protective factor.

Speaking of feeling competent, let's talk about Self-Determination Theory. This is a theory in psychology that presents a framework for understanding human motivation. This theory argues that people are motivated by both extrinsic and intrinsic rewards and that the three key rewards in motivation are competence, autonomy, and relatedness. When these three things are present, people are more motivated, which also makes them feel better mentally and socially, persist through challenges, and experience improvements in both performance and creativity. When people lack any of these three motivations, they experience negative mental health consequences. We've already seen one way in which gaming can foster competence. A 2006 paper on the topic argues that gaming can also foster autonomy (in that you can make a lot of independent decisions in the game) as well as relatedness through teamwork. Thus, gaming has the potential to offer great levels of motivation, which in turn can lead to improved mental health. That said, it's important to note that the same paper found that people who play the games obsessively are less likely to reap these rewards, so when game play heads toward addiction, the costs may outweigh the benefits.

However, we have to be careful when making assumptions about those costs and benefits. For example, it's easy to assume that if you enter a dissociative state when gaming, then that's always a bad thing. But a 2010 study published in *Culture, Medicine, and Psychiatry* found that when *World of Warcraft* players get so immersed in their game play as to "induce dissociative states in which players attribute dimensions of self and experience to in-game characters," it has the potential to actually benefit the player's well-being. Many of the benefits found in this study associated with being in a flow state, not the least of which was stress reduction. Ultimately, they found that whether these immersive states were positive or negative depended on whether the individual used gaming to reduce stress or gaming was likely to cause them stress. Thus, whether gaming specifically, and Internet use more generally, is negative or positive depends significantly on the individual. Even what looks like a problem generally may not be problematic for a specific individual. That's why it's helpful to go back to the definition of Internet addiction that includes the aspect of causing harm or negative repercussions in life; constant game play may not be a problem if it's not causing harm. For some people, it may even be beneficial.

One interesting area of exploration is the use of video games to assist with pain management. Immersion in a video game can help reduce or even eradicate chronic pain. The game *SnowWorld*, for example, was created specifically as a nonopioid form of pain management for particular use in the military and in burn treatment. Gaming releases not just dopamine but also endorphins that can help protect against pain. People who for any reason don't want to utilize a substance such as morphine can sometimes reap the same pain management benefits from gaming. Of course, that itself could turn into an addiction, so there are pros and cons, but it can certainly be a short-term benefit if not one useful in the long term.

ACCESSING THERAPY ONLINE

We can't talk about the potential mental health benefits of the Internet without talking about the fact that today it is used as a medium for therapy. People use the Internet to find therapists and to get therapeutic advice. People also seek social support, which sometimes looks a lot like group therapy, through forums, social media, and other aspects of the Internet. More directly, people can access therapy services with educated and licensed professionals whom they meet with online. Sometimes online therapy is an adjunct to in-person therapy; other times people complete their entire therapeutic experience online only. Online therapy usually takes place over video to allow for as much face-to-face communication as possible. However, it's also possible to have voice-only therapy, and sometimes people even get therapy or therapeutic support through text messages and voice messages. It's an emerging field, and one that changes rapidly, so we are only just beginning to understand the pros and cons.

Overall, therapy is a helpful supportive tool for people in many situations, and online therapy is no exception. Like with all aspects of the Internet, it seems to provide the most benefit when it is a supplement to, instead of a replacement for, in-person connection. That said, just like in the cases of isolation described earlier, online therapy is better than nothing for people who can't access in-person therapy for one reason or another. Online therapy tends to be low cost (although it may or may not be covered by your insurance). It makes therapy, particularly more niche forms of therapy, available to people in small towns and rural areas where they might not be able to access the same services in person. People who are housebound due to agoraphobia, paranoia, another mental health issue, or a physical limitation may find that online therapy is their only viable therapeutic option. People who travel frequently, or couples who are currently in a long-distance relationship, may be able to keep therapy appointments more regularly when online therapy is an option.

Online therapy might be particularly valuable for someone who is in immediate crisis. When you're in crisis—feeling suicidal, for example—it's critical that you get help immediately. Depending on where you are and what kind of professional support you already have in place, that help may or may not be easy to access. For example, if you already have a therapist whom you see regularly, then you may be able to call that therapist and get in for an immediate appointment. On the other hand, if you don't have a therapist and you aren't even sure how you would pay for one, trying to get help in the midst of a mental health crisis can feel almost impossible. Oftentimes people resort to calling a hotline, which is really a form of online or phone therapy, and the person there may suggest that they go to the emergency room for immediate help. While that might be a good solution for some, it's not for others. The option of online therapy for crisis situations becomes a good one. If you need help immediately and a licensed therapist is on the other end of your computer at any time of day or night, then they can help you during your crisis.

Crisis intervention is only one type of therapy. Another type of therapy that seems to work well in the online world is cognitive behavioral therapy (CBT). This is a popular type of therapy that helps you better understand your thoughts and actions and learn new coping mechanisms. It's been found to be an effective treatment option for many mental health issues including anxiety disorders and substance use. Since it is effective for substance addiction, it has the potential to be beneficial for people struggling

with Internet addiction. Research so far indicates that there may be no difference in the success of CBT when received as online therapy versus in
person. Someone may be able to visit an online therapist or one in person
and get the same results when it comes to the benefits of this particular
form of treatment. In comparison, if your personality and mental health
issue are better treated by something such as somatic therapy or relational
therapy, then you might not benefit from online therapy because you need
that in-person touch and communication style.

Some people find that online therapy is a good "first step" for them
when they've never tried therapy before. Going to therapy for the first time
can be intimidating. If you're coping with social anxiety, or you struggle
to let down your guard with people in person, or you simply aren't sure
whether or not therapy is right for you, then you might put a toe in the
water by trying out online therapy first. If you have a positive experience,
then you benefit immediately from that and may also decide that you want
to go to in-person therapy as a next step, which offers additional benefits.
If a person wouldn't have gotten therapy any other way for whatever reason, then online therapy is a good solution. Whether the benefits outweigh
drawbacks for other people is up for debate.

Pros and Cons of the Internet for Education

One of the arguments commonly made for technology is that it can
be used by children to enhance education. It's an interactive, educational
tool, after all (or at least it can be), but according to Nicholas Kardaras,
"There is not one credible research study that shows that a child exposed
to more technology earlier in life has better educational outcomes than
a tech-free kid; while there is some evidence that screen exposed kids
may have some increased pattern-recognition abilities, there just isn't any
research that shows that they become better students or better learners."
This doesn't necessarily mean that technology and the Internet can't be
beneficial to students; it means that on its own the Internet isn't an educational tool. It's all about how we use it, so changes need to be made to
educate children (and their parents and teachers) about ways to utilize the
Internet that enhance their existing skills and improve their educational
outcomes rather than serving as a substitute for other skills.

Consider the scenario of learning language from a dictionary. In the
olden days of the twentieth century, when a child was reading a book and
came across a word that they didn't know, the way to find out (other than
asking an adult) was to check out a dictionary. That action is still the same

today, and doing so is much simpler thanks to at-our-fingertips technology. There is no need to stop reading, search the house for where the dictionary is, find the right page, and read the word. But, while it's more convenient to do a quick online search on your phone for the meaning of a word, is it as effective? The entire process of finding the word in the dictionary may lend itself better to actually remembering the meaning of the word that you learn than the quick look-it-up Internet option. When you look up a word on the Internet, or ask Siri for the definition, you see what it means and then quickly move on to something else, and usually that word falls out of your memory. The tangible multistep action (and the more dedicated intent to learn) that comes with looking the word up in your desktop print dictionary can help to solidify the meaning of that word in your memory.

Does this mean that you can't learn language through reading and looking up the words that you don't know in an Internet dictionary? Of course not. What it means is that we have to be more intentional about our actions, noticing that this is a word we want to learn and taking the extra steps to learn it. This means not just looking up the word on the Internet but taking the time to write the word down along with its meaning, maybe use it in a sentence or write out the context in which we found the word and go back to it again to keep reminding ourselves of what it means until it's locked into our memory. If we use the Internet only as a shortcut, then it may not offer benefits, but that doesn't mean it doesn't have the potential to be a great thing.

Creating a vocabulary list on your phone and setting a phone reminder to review it regularly can be just as effective as using index cards to learn new words. It is all about setting the intention and the behaviors that support that intention, whether we do that with technology or not. It's just that in today's Internet-dominated world, it becomes much easier to mindlessly look up the word, see what it means for the moment that you need it, and promptly forget its meaning moments later. That can happen when looking up a word in the physical dictionary as well, but the effort put in to find the word gives you the time and focus to solidify your intention to learn the word. If you can find ways to slow down your Internet use long enough to set and meet that intention, then the technology can serve the same purpose.

Of course, this is just one example of the Internet as it applies to education. This is really a very broad discussion. It ranges from whether or not kids should use technology in the classroom (and if so, how much of the time and in what ways) to the potential benefits and drawbacks of an online-only education. If kids are ignoring the teacher because they're watching funny memes on their phones during class time, then that's a negative, but if the teacher uses a funny meme at the start of a lecture to capture the kids' attention, then it can be a positive. If a child drops out of school because of bullying, then attending an online-only program might be the best option, but if a child never has to face the outside world because they're able to do their entire education online, then that could be problematic. Like many aspects of the conversation around where we're going with technology as a society, this is a huge topic that we can't fully address here.

One issue that's specifically relevant to mental health is the growing problem of attention disorders. Children who are exposed to a lot of screen time, and certainly those children who develop a full-blown addiction to the Internet, seem to have problems with attention that relate to those changes in the brain discussed in previous chapters. Many of the teachers I've spoken to say that in their own experience, attention levels have decreased dramatically in recent years and they believe that technology is at least partially to blame. If children aren't able to pay attention in a classroom, then they aren't able to learn as well. But if technology can be utilized in positive ways in the classroom, then perhaps it can mitigate some of that harm. It's a controversy that our society is still in the early stages of sorting out.

CAN THE INTERNET HELP SOLVE THE PROBLEM OF INTERNET ADDICTION?

The Internet is here to stay (at least until technology advances again and replaces itself with something else). So, one course of action is to utilize the power of our technology for good. We can use the Internet itself to help mitigate the negatives of Internet use. Perhaps we can even use the Internet to resolve Internet addiction.

In terms of minimizing harm, there are numerous apps and tools now available to help people who are concerned about overusing the Internet. At a very basic level, we can easily research the problem of Internet addiction and come to find solutions, as well as peer support and perhaps even professional support, through the Internet itself. If you think that you or someone you love might have a problem with Internet addiction, one of the first things that you might do is head to Google or ask Alexa to tell you more about Internet addiction. This is one of the simplest ways in which the Internet itself can help battle the problems of using the Internet.

Once you determine that either you have an addiction or you want to limit your Internet use so as to reduce the risk of developing an addiction, you can implement a variety of safeguards. In the earlier chapter on treatment options for Internet addiction, we saw that a harm reduction approach means that most people are going to use the Internet to some degree but will limit that use in various ways. They will reduce their use to specific tools, limit their time on devices, or do both of those things. Our technology now comes with built-in tools and easy-to-download apps to help facilitate that self-limitation. (Parents can also use those same tools to limit children.)

When Apple released the iOS 12 update for its devices, it came with a new feature called Screen Time. This means that anyone who has an up-to-date iPhone, iPad, or other Apple device can not only see how much time they're on the device but also easily limit themselves based on that information. Screen Time allows you to see the following:

- How many minutes you've spent on your phone today and across the past seven days
- What time of day you were using those minutes (so you know what else you were doing at the time)
- How many minutes were spent on different applications such as messaging, a particular game, and Facebook
- How many times you picked up your phone and what application you first used upon picking it up
- How many notifications you received, the average per hour, and which apps sent you those notifications
- Whether that's an increase or decrease in your usage compared to the prior week

This gives you a lot of information that can help you see what features of your device might be addictive for you personally. You can alter the settings to include all of your devices or just one. Moreover, you can use the app to schedule "downtime" (time when you don't want the screen to work) as well as time limits for each app and specific content/privacy restrictions. So, if you see that you overuse Facebook, especially at lunchtime, you can put a limit on your daily Facebook use and also schedule downtime at lunchtime to make sure you aren't using up your limit then. You can easily turn these things on and off. If you have a full-blown addiction, that ease is a problem because you can quickly resume your problematic use. But if you're in the early stages of problematic use, tools like this can help you regain control over your Internet use so that it's working for you instead of against you.

This built-in iPhone app is just one of many examples. There are many similar apps available to monitor and limit use of your phones, tablets, and computers. There are also many other types of apps and software programs that have the potential to help limit online distractions so that you can reap the benefits of the Internet without engaging in the more addictive properties. For example, you can look for Zenware, which is a category of software that helps restrict usage during certain activities. One great example is WriteRoom, which blocks out your whole screen so that all you see is the text that you're writing (green text on a black background that harkens back to the early days of computer technology), allowing you to focus on deep thought and writing without any of the tempting distractions of other tabs and windows. Similarly, Ommwriter turns off email and chat notifications and also allows you to choose one of three calming backgrounds that were specifically chosen by a color therapist to allow for relaxation.

The Internet has the potential to cause addiction for some people. But it also has a lot of benefits, and the Internet itself can provide solutions to addiction. One of the scariest things about Internet addiction is that the technology has advanced so quickly that we are changing our daily behaviors, and potentially our brains, in the blink of an eye. But one of the most amazing things is that as fast as we're seeing problems, we're using both technology and the connectivity to others that the Internet allows to identify and resolve those problems.

CHAPTER 10

What Are the Implications of New and Emerging Technologies?

The first iPhone launched in 2007. Prior to that, some people had smartphones. BlackBerry was the most common brand, and it had its own potential for addiction (the term "CrackBerry" was bandied about). But it wasn't until after the launch of the iPhone that we began to really see everyone around us using them all of the time. In terms of global history, the Internet is young, and smartphones and social media are even younger. And yet, new technologies are emerging every day. Things that we are only just starting to see right now—like self-driving cars and lifelike smart robots—are going to be ubiquitous before we know it. There will also be other technologies that perhaps we can't even fathom right now. What are the implications of these new and emerging technologies for Internet addiction? We can only guess.

There are so many different new and emerging technologies. A short list includes artificial intelligence (AI), augmented and virtual reality, biometrics and implanted chip technology, blockchain, cryptocurrency, Dark Net sites, drones, edge computing (a variation of cloud computing), improved haptic response, robots (including sex robots), self-driving vehicles, smart home technologies, targeted advertising, voice assistants (Alexa and Siri), and 3D printing. We can imagine so many different scenarios in which each of these things might help or hinder problems of Internet addiction. For example, if it becomes the norm that we implant technology directly into our bodies, how is that going to affect the brain, and can we do something with that technology to maximize the benefits without leading to more addiction? This isn't the realm of science fiction; it's technology that's emerging here and now. That said, for all of our guesses, we can't say for sure where any of this is going, yet. For the purposes of this book, we'll explore only two particular aspects of this new and emerging technology: augmented and virtual reality and AI.

AUGMENTED AND VIRTUAL REALITY

We are right on the cusp of a huge change in technology thanks to developments in virtual reality, and we've already seen some of that when it comes to augmented reality. Augmented reality is when you view the real world through a screen and see something on the screen that isn't there in real life. Virtual reality is when you look only at a screen (usually through glasses or headsets) and immerse yourself entirely into the world there, sometimes with additional sensory input from haptics to make it feel even more like you're in that world.

We'll discuss augmented reality first. Not that long ago, some friends visited here from out of town with their three children, all under the age of twelve. San Francisco is a fascinating city, with not only rich history and architecture but also really fun, colorful characters and activities. I was curious what the kids were enjoying most about this fabulous city that they were visiting for the first time. The five-year-old barely glanced up from his screen as he answered, "There are so many Pokemon here." *Pokemon Go* was one of the first augmented reality games to really hit the mainstream and start a craze. In this game, you look at the real world through your phone screen, and various little Pokemon creatures pop up on the screen. You have to navigate around the real world to find and collect them. On the plus side, the kid was out in the real world, moving his body around and avoiding some of the negatives associated with a sedentary life. On the other hand, he didn't seem to see this rich city around him because he was narrowly focused on finding the Pokemon.

The augmented reality game became so popular that psychologists (and others) almost immediately began questioning whether it was a positive or a negative for mental health. On the positive side, people were moving around in the fresh air, which reduced depression and anxiety. In some cases, it encouraged social engagement with people in the real world, which was a further benefit. Plus, it had some of the benefits of gaming such as the feeling of competence when achieving a new goal by catching a new Pokemon. On the other hand, if you're engaging with your phone instead of the people around you, then you're risking some of those same problems (loneliness that begets depression, etc.). Plus, you run the risk of addiction, and if you get addicted to the game, then there are more negatives than positives. Fifty-two-year-old Dominic Rushe shared in an article in the *Guardian* about a time when he ignored warnings to evacuate an area and risked his life in a lightning storm because he wanted to capture a Pokemon in a particular area. This sounds ridiculous, but reports indicate that there was a spike in distracted driving accidents right after the launch of *Pokemon Go*; people were paying attention to the augmented reality instead of the actual reality of the road. If you're risking your real-world physical health and safety, then you're dealing with addiction. If augmented reality helps you engage with the real world, that's a benefit; if it helps you escape the real world even when you're out in it, then that's a risk.

Virtual reality takes you completely out of the physical world, immersing you into the virtual world. It looks and feels like you're in a completely different place. If you're in virtual reality and it looks like a hole opens up in front of you, in the real life you will jump back because it feels real.

You can be a completely different person in virtual reality. The same problems that we see when it comes to prolonged Internet use may get exacerbated with virtual reality. For example, consider the rare but problematic issue of psychosis among people with Internet addiction. Prolonged gaming, in particular, can lead to a break with reality where the person doesn't know that they aren't in the game anymore. Virtual reality allows games to become even more realistic, which can increase the potential for confusing the brain as to what's real and what's not, thereby risking the problem of increased likelihood of psychosis.

Highly immersive technology increases the risks of our existing technology. The more immersive the technologies get, not only the more potential harms but also the more potential benefits. Consider when augmented and/or virtual reality becomes a regular part of social media experiences. A highly immersive social media interaction with peers and support groups might greatly enhance their benefits, offering more of the positives associated with "real life" experiences while also negating some of the problems that the limitations of social media currently incur. If you feel like you're "really there" with people, then perhaps you'll feel more empathy online instead of less (as is often the case today). On the other hand, if you use virtual reality to create an avatar that's not anything like yourself, you risk greater self-dislike, more problems with your own identity, and increased likelihood of falling into catfishing behavior.

Likewise, consider the implications of virtual reality when it comes to pornography. If online porn is addictive, then virtual reality porn has the potential to be even more addictive. It stimulates more of the brain. If you would rather engage in virtual porn with a stranger than spend time with your partner, then that's likely to cause significant problems in your relationship. In contrast, though, if virtual reality pornography can be made to incorporate some sense of "real person" feedback that makes you feel like you're actually interacting with another human and have to be sensitive to their needs and feelings, then there's the potential that it could reduce some of the numbing sensation that online pornography today seems to cause. It could go either way, and only time will tell which way it's going to go. How it plays out will also vary from person to person.

Like with most aspects of the Internet, augmented reality and virtual reality both have the potential for either good or harm. One benefit, for example, is that some people may actually develop better self-esteem when playing with an avatar that looks better than they do in real life. This is counterintuitive and may not be true for all people, because there's always the risk that you won't be satisfied with your real life self and therefore have higher risk of addiction since you're more comfortable in the game. However, Pang reports that Jeremy Bailenson of VR Lab has done some convincing studies that people playing with better-looking avatars have better self-esteem even when they are not playing the game.

Augmented and virtual reality may have naturally protective benefits that help to reduce problems with addiction. They may also have built-in features that increase the likelihood of addiction. How that plays out from person to person, and across society as a whole, is something yet to be seen. Because we know about the potential harms of Internet addiction, we as a society have the ability to look forward to these new technologies with a wiser eye and hopefully design them and utilize them in ways that are more positive.

One important thing to note as a potential positive is the role that augmented and virtual reality can play in mental health treatment. Virtual reality offers sensory feedback and allows you to deeply immerse yourself into experiences that feel very real but that you also know aren't real. This combination of features makes it helpful in certain types of mental health care. Research indicates that it can be particularly effective when used in therapy for people with posttraumatic stress disorder (PTSD). It's also been shown to have positive outcomes for people dealing with phobias, social anxiety, and certain types of paranoia.

Some mental health issues just don't respond that well to traditional talk therapy. Trauma, including PTSD, is one of the biggest ones. Many people find that it's not helpful to talk about the traumatic experience. At worst, it can trigger negative reminders that make the symptoms of trauma even worse. Even when it's not harmful, though, it's not particularly helpful. That's why PTSD is often treated with alternative therapies including animal therapy and somatic therapy. Virtual reality can also be helpful.

It's been used specifically with military veterans who suffer from PTSD. They use immersive virtual reality to return to the war zone where they can physically work through the situations that caused the trauma in the first place. While at first glance you might think that would be more traumatizing, research indicates that many veterans find it helpful—being able to control the situation in a new way through virtual reality while in the company and supportive care of a therapist helps them to heal.

People with anxiety, including phobias, can also benefit from virtual reality. One of the most effective treatment for phobias (and one also used for obsessive compulsive disorder [OCD]) is exposure and response prevention. In this treatment, the therapist exposes you to the things that trigger your fear, and you prevent yourself from engaging in the negative response. For example, if you have a fear of spiders, the therapist might have you hold a spider, and you work to breathe through the fear instead of running away. Virtual reality provides a way to offer more immersive exposure experiences while also placing the individual at less actual risk. Someone can work on their fear of spiders or heights without having to actually hold a spider or climb up on a ledge. People who have social anxiety can practice being with others and communicating in a virtual setting that feels very real. Of course, the goal of this therapy would be to eventually translate that to the outside world; if the individual is limited only to virtual relationships, then the problem isn't resolved. But it can be a huge stepping stone in therapy.

And we're just beginning to scratch the surface as to how virtual reality might help in the therapy room. For example, some very early research indicates that it can help in concrete ways with symptoms of depression. One of the problems in depression is that you lose interest in things and feel numb; a therapist might help you through virtual reality by exposing you to immersive experiences that reignite some of your interests again. If you feel more excited about things again, then you can start to do more, which means that you can start engaging in treatments that further help you resolve your depression. But this is all new. We don't know yet how it will all play out. Virtual reality could help resolve some types of depression, but it could also cause depression in the same way that existing forms of Internet addiction seem to cause depression for some people. Consider, for example, if your depression is linked with loneliness. If you use virtual reality to connect with others in meaningful ways, then it could ease your symptoms, but if you use virtual reality to escape and not deal with the problem, then it could exacerbate your symptoms.

One way that people might benefit mentally from virtual reality is through the use of immersive meditation experiences. Mindfulness practice is increasingly popular as a treatment for a variety of mental health issues. It's challenging for some people to sit still and practice mindfulness on their own, so guided meditation is a great way to get started. If you're sitting in your room trying to do guided meditation through an app, then there are a lot of potential distractions. If, on the other hand, you're immersed in a virtual world that's guiding you into meditation, then that could be a benefit. Therapists are working on ways that they can incorporate mindfulness, de-stressing, and centering/grounding practices into their therapy through virtual reality.

Limbix and Psious are just two of many virtual reality companies that focus specifically on creating tools for therapists to utilize in their sessions. They both have products that offer entryways into mindfulness and breathing practice. They also have tools to help with various types of anxiety and phobias. For example, they both offer their own versions of a virtual reality bar scenario in which you can learn to overcome social anxiety by practicing sitting at the bar and speaking with people. Some of the other specific anxiety-provoking situations they offer include taking an exam, getting a shot from a needle, and flying on an airplane. People who have serious anxiety could work through that fear in therapy. And we can imagine that these tools could also help the average person without serious mental health issues, like the child who might be flying for the first time or afraid to go to the doctor and get that shot.

Virtual reality isn't just a benefit in the physical therapy room but could also enhance the benefits of online therapy. One of the biggest limitations of online therapy is that you're missing that personal touch of being present one-on-one with your therapist. If you and your therapist both enter a virtual reality world together, then you mitigate some of that. Someone who can't access therapy due to cost or location can reap the benefits of a face-to-face talk in a therapy room using virtual reality.

One of the things we looked at in the previous chapter was whether the technology itself can help resolve the problems of technology. We can ask more specifically, is it possible to use augmented and/or virtual reality to solve Internet addiction? There is a very promising study published in the June 2016 issue of *Computer Methods and Programs in Biomedicine* that suggests it's possible. The researchers found that virtual reality therapy could actually improve areas of the brain affected by online gaming addiction. They specifically found that use of virtual reality as a form of therapy helped balance the cortico-striatal-limbic circuit of the brain, reducing the severity of online gaming addiction. They compared their virtual reality method with traditional cognitive behavioral therapy (CBT) and found that it produced comparable results. In other words, someone with a gaming addiction could go to traditional CBT, or they could use virtual reality therapy to resolve the problem of online gaming addiction.

Virtual reality has been found to be a helpful treatment for other types of addiction as well. There has been specific research into the use of virtual reality therapy for nicotine addiction, and it points to great success. People in recovery are traditionally at great risk of developing other addictions, including Internet addiction. If we can figure out a way to utilize virtual reality during the recovery process as a positive thing instead of a potential tool for more addiction, then it could turn out to be a great thing. For that to happen, the makers of the technology have to have an interest in the positive use of their technology, and one strong motivator is the marketplace, so we as buyers have to put our money toward those more positive uses particularly when it comes to the new and emerging technologies such as augmented and virtual reality.

ARTIFICIAL INTELLIGENCE

We use the term a lot, but what does "artificial intelligence" really mean? Put very simply, it refers to machines (computers) that respond in ways that are consistent with how humans respond. A 2018 Brookings report suggests that AI systems have three key qualities: intentionality, intelligence, and adaptability. Intentionality means that they can make decisions based on real-time data without being limited to preprogrammed responses. For example, autonomous (self-driving) cars have to be able to respond to whatever happens on the road in the moment. Intelligence means that AI systems utilize machine learning and data analytics to respond in ways that consider complex issues such as bias and justice. Adaptability means that the computer is able to keep on learning, adjusting, and improving upon itself as conditions change.

Autonomous vehicles are one example of AI in action today. Here in San Francisco they're on the road regularly. I frequently see them waiting at four-way stops as they seem to be "thinking" about what to do next. They're a little bit clumsy right now. I imagine that the driver inside has to take over now and then. But they're getting better every day. It causes a lot of controversy. Some people are terrified of the idea of machines taking over the planet. Do you want to be in a car that's driving itself and decides to take you somewhere that you don't want to go? Or that gets hacked by someone with bad intentions? (Of course, even the cars we drive ourselves are computer based today, so it doesn't have to be a self-driving car to have hacking as a potential risk.) Trusting a car to drive itself may seem a little crazy, but is it crazier than trusting all of the other humans on the road? Especially when most of those humans are now distracted by their devices, among other distractions? Whether you are for, against, or neutral about autonomous vehicles, they're here, and they're a great example of AI in society today.

If you can't quite get a mental grasp on the self-driving car, though, consider a different type of AI that many people use daily: voice-activated personal assistants like Alexa and Siri. We say, "Hey, Siri," and then we ask the device to answer questions, set timers, or perform calculations. If Alexa is linked with your home's other smart technology, then the options for what you can ask the device to do open up even more. As these tools keep learning, they'll be able to do more and more.

Okay, but how does all of this relate to Internet addiction? Darren Austin, writing for Business Insider, makes a great argument for how devices like Alexa have some of the same built-in addictive qualities as other aspects of the Internet. He uses the hooked model, which is author Nir Eyal's description of how technology hooks us (remember, we explored this back in Chapter 3), to explain how his own behavior with Alexa has some of the warning signs of addiction. The hooked model starts with a trigger—external as well as internal. One of the biggest triggers for Internet addiction is a negative feeling; you want to escape feeling bad, so you engage in the addictive behavior. Austin noticed that every time he felt the uncomfortable feeling of uncertainty, he'd quickly turn to the reassuring voice of Alexa. Asking her for the answer relieved the feeling, and asking is the second step in the hooked model. The easier it is to perform the action, the more addictive the technology is likely to become, and asking Alexa is much easier than even doing a quick Google search on your phone.

The next part of the hooked model is that part of addiction that we're very familiar with by now—the reward. You get the immediate reward of getting your answer from Alexa. But Austin points out that it's more than that. Sometimes these devices respond in a clever or funny way. That surprises us. It feels good. It might offer that dopamine hit. It's not all of the time, so it's an intermittent reward, and we are primed to love that. And Austin also points out that sometimes Alexa is wrong—or she doesn't give us the answer we want—and that in itself means that getting the right answer from her is another intermittent reward. It's annoying to say, "Alexa, turn on the room light" and get no response, but when she finally gets it right, we get the reward.

And finally, as we know, we are more likely to become addicted to technology when we invest time, energy, money, and the like into the device. With Alexa, you're constantly teaching her new things. You might take the time to download a new skill for her to use, or you might let her know what your favorite restaurant is. As she learns, you're becoming more invested, which makes you more prone to addiction.

For the addict, this could mean preferring Alexa over human interaction. One blogger, Kathy Gottberg, noted that she felt like her husband was more interested in Alexa than in her, and when she asked what he liked so much about her, he basically responded, "She does what I want and doesn't talk back." We can get instant gratification from our devices without having to deal with the messy interaction that other humans cause us. That's one of the problems of social media, as we know, but at least on some level we know that somewhere on the other end of the social media app is another human being. With Alexa, we know no such thing, which has the potential to further reduce empathy and increase the problems of social isolation.

Consider as these technologies come together in the form of very life-like robots, including sex robots. Using virtual reality and haptic feedback, you can begin to feel like your robot is as real as any human. But she'll respond, like Alexa, mostly only in the ways that you want. What potential risk does this create for humans who are already having trouble bonding with others? We don't know. The technological advances that we are just beginning to see could mitigate some of the problems of Internet addiction, or it could make them worse. How we proceed individually and as a society could help determine the difference.

CHAPTER 11

Whose Responsibility Is It to Resolve Internet Addiction?

This brings us to the final big controversy in the topic of Internet addiction: whose problem is it to resolve? If we agree that some forms of technology have a risk of Internet addiction and that certain populations are at potential risk of that addiction, then whose job is it to solve that problem? Like all of our problems in society, it's not an easy question to answer. How you feel about it is affected not only by who you think is most to blame but also by your views on such things as the role of government in individual lives and the importance of personal responsibility.

For example, if you believe in limiting government involvement as much as possible, then the role of the government in resolving Internet addiction will be smaller for you than for someone who believes the government should be involved in handling societal issues. If you believe that addiction is an individual issue, then you're more likely to think that addicts and their parents should resolve the issue than someone who looks at the intersectionality of the many causes of addiction and finds that perhaps institutions must play a bigger role. These are all huge questions, and there are no simple solutions. But by starting the conversation about the different roles that various people and organizations can play, we can start to come up with new ways that we can benefit from the advances in technology while mitigating some of the addictive harms.

THE ROLE OF THE INDIVIDUAL

Picture a heroin addict in active addiction. What responsibility does that person have to take care of their addiction alone? Now imagine that the heroin addict is only fourteen years old. Does that change how much responsibility you think that person must take as compared to how much involvement there should be from parents, schools, and authorities? How much should the government offer in terms of support and care to stop the addiction, and how much should the person have to be responsible for? As we know from substance addiction, there's no easy equation for distributing "blame" or coming up with a solution. It's no different with Internet addiction. We may be tempted to think that the individual should just put the phone down, but addiction is more complicated than that.

When it comes to individual responsibility for dealing with Internet addiction, there are two types of individuals: the addicts themselves and parents of (potential) addicts. Parents are tasked with the huge responsibility of setting rules around device use in their homes. Children are at greater risk of addiction than adults because their brains are still developing. But there is no blueprint for what a parent should do to help their children thrive in a tech-dominated society while still avoiding addiction.

And, as author Anya Kamenetz highlights, there is more intersectionality than you might guess at first. In other words, not all parents are on an even playing field. A very simple example that she gives is that if you're an upper-middle-class parent who pays a nanny a lot of money to engage in analog activities with your child, then you have a lot more control over whether or not they use devices in your absence than does the lower-income parent who has to ask a neighbor for the favor of watching the kids while she goes to work. Similarly, if you're in a two-parent home with an only child and one of you is a stay-at-home parent, then perhaps you're more likely to be able to provide your child with nonscreen engagement and activities than the single, working parent with four children who might give their children screens just to get enough quiet in the house to get dinner on the table. The lower-income or busy working parent is not at fault; it's simply a difference that we have to notice in our society. Individuals, including parents, can and should play a huge role in setting boundaries that limit the risks of Internet addiction, but we also have to recognize that not all individuals are in the same circumstances, and so there are varying levels of ability to be able to set such limits.

And, even when you can set boundaries for yourself and your children, it's hard to know what those boundaries should be. We are all new at this. The research is young, the technology is changing quickly, and we're just beginning to get a grasp on what Internet addiction might look like. Perhaps the best the individual can do is just try.

We can look closely at what kind of relationship we have with our devices. What do you like about your use? What causes problems? Learn the signs of addiction, and determine whether or not you see those cropping up in your own life. As a parent, pay attention to how your children act when they use their devices more as compared to less—or when they experience certain content as compared with other types of information online. Pay attention, ask questions, tweak usage, and see what happens. In particular, be curious, but vigilant, when adding new technologies to your life. Whether it's a new device, a new app, or simply a new feature of one of those things, take the time to think carefully about it. It's easier to prevent an addiction than to interrupt one, so take the time to be thoughtful about how you incorporate new things into your life. Research seems to indicate that balancing screen time with active engagement in real life (including hands-on activities and in-person relationships) is one simple, effective starting point.

On the one hand, individuals have a great capacity for controlling their usage (and to some extent, that of their children). On the other hand, beating yourself up for not being perfect at it doesn't help the situation. As we know, bad feelings make us even more likely to turn to addictive behavior. So, we have to strike a balance here. The individual does have a huge amount of personal responsibility to take, but there's also only so much the individual can do.

THE ROLE OF INSTITUTIONS AND GOVERNMENT

There are two big questions that provoke a lot of smaller questions: what role should the individual play in stopping Internet addiction and what role should institutions and government agencies play? And these aren't necessarily easy to separate. Consider, for example, the role that schools should play as well as the potential role of the individual teacher. These are very different things, and there are no clear-cut answers. But we can at least ask the questions about what different groups, and individuals within those groups, can do to be aware of and help prevent or resolve Internet addiction.

Role of Schools

Schools play a huge role today in identifying problems for at-risk children as well as in educating children and their parents about risks. They also have to grapple with the huge questions of when and how technology should be used in the classroom. Different schools are addressing this in different ways. Kamenetz has identified three common types of classrooms today (in so far as tech goes):

1. The paperless classroom, which means that the teacher uses technology (often Google Apps for Education) to perform common classroom tasks from grading papers to marking down behavioral

problems. Gone are the days when the disruptive child's name went up on the board with tally marks to indicate how many minutes of detention they'd get because all of that happens on computers today. Parents can stay connected with daily updates, and both parents and kids can see homework, grades, and notes online.

2. Rotation stations, which means that children spend part of the day on devices, often doing activities at their own pace. When I was in school, this was called "going to the computer lab," and sometimes it still looks that way, but more often the children are on mobile devices in their regular classrooms.

3. Distraction derbies, which are tech-enabled classrooms where children spend all or most of the day on their devices engaging in what may be classwork or may be social media, games, chatting, and so forth. They may use school-provided devices, their own devices brought from home, or a combination of both.

Schools are still figuring out how best to implement technology in the classroom, and it can look any of these ways. There are some great advantages to tech in the classroom. A busy teacher with too many students can have each student work at their own pace on their devices while attending one-on-one to students who have special needs, and they can perhaps more efficiently identify those needs with computer feedback than they could when they had to grade every paper by hand. But if children are at risk of Internet addiction, then having more screen time in the classroom has to be considered a potential risk. What should schools be doing to mitigate that risk? Should teachers be educated in the warning signs of Internet addiction, and if they see those signs, what should they do?

So, the question of the role of schools is twofold: (1) how should schools incorporate technology in the classroom with an understanding of and respect for the risks of Internet addiction among children and (2) what responsibility do schools have to identify, prevent, and raise awareness about Internet addiction. Those are huge questions. And they don't even take into consideration the way that the answers might trickle down and affect individuals—not just students but also teachers, principals, and school counselors. We don't have the answers, but it's important that we are thinking about these things.

Role of the Media

The 2018 movie *Ready Player One* depicts a possibly near future in which intensity in the virtual world bleeds over into violence in the real world, but it also speaks to the potential for merging the two worlds in a positive way. At the end of this film, the hero and heroine take over the virtual world, and they make the controversial decision to shut off access to that world on Tuesdays and Thursdays. They do this based on the sage advice of the game's creator who has shown them that no matter how amazing virtual reality gets, it is no comparison to "real reality." Viewers hear this announcement as a narrative over a visual of the couple happily cuddling and kissing in their real world, despite the fact that their virtual avatar characters are arguably sexier and more exciting than the flesh-and-blood selves. This is a great example of how media itself can highlight the pros and cons of choices in technology and encourage people of all ages to get off the screen and out into the real world to experience real kisses, real connections, and real feelings.

The media can and does highlight the risks of Internet addiction and other problems associated with technology. (And, of course, the Internet is itself "the media.") *Ready Player One* is just one example. Another is the television/Netflix show *Black Mirror* that depicts a variety of different near-future scenarios related to problems associated with technology. Television and other forms of entertainment make commentary on social issues, and the topic of Internet addiction is no exception. But what responsibility, if any, does the media have to help resolve the issue? Given the importance of free speech, we can't—and shouldn't—mandate what messages media should share. We should, perhaps, make sure that all voices in the debate can be heard.

Notably, there are limitations on media already. The movie rating system, for example, prevents (at least theoretically) children under a certain age from viewing specific types of content. There's a similar system in place for gaming content. These systems are arguably flawed, but they offer one way that media companies share responsibility for regulating content for children. Could we eventually put a system in place that warns about how addictive certain content might be? Research indicates, for example, that people can become addicted to a game as simple as *Tetris*, but they are significantly more likely to become addicted to a game like *World of Warcraft*, so could those games have different ratings based not just on content but also on risk for addiction?

Media also comes with warning labels besides ratings. Television shows with graphic content warn that "viewer discretion is advised." Increasingly, we even see trigger warnings at the start of online articles. Media is letting people know, "Hey, there's something here, and you might want to see it, but you also might want to think twice because it could have a negative impact on your wellbeing and/or mental health." The individual gets the choice, but the media gives them additional information to help them make that choice. Could the media do something similar with not just the content but also how the content relates to addiction? "Some people who view this content regularly find themselves developing Internet addiction. Viewer discretion is advised."

Role of Other Businesses

Media companies certainly aren't the only types of businesses or content producers that might bear some responsibility for the issue of widespread Internet addiction. Tech companies, for example, play a crucial role in creating the tools that are leading to the addiction. What role should they have to play in resolving the problem? Many individuals have come out of these companies to raise awareness about the issue. If you read widely about Internet addiction, then you'll almost certainly come across the name Tristan Harris. He was a design ethicist at Google who became well known for a 140+ slide presentation he created in-house called "A Call to Minimize Distraction & Respect Users' Attention." In it, he warned that Google and other big companies were engaging in behavior that was addicting their users and that they should take responsibility for that. He went on to launch the Time Well Spent movement and founded the Center for Humane Technology, and he continues to speak about the problem of Internet addiction, including the risks of emerging technologies, and the role that the companies creating this technology have to play in mitigating the problem.

Part of the mission of the Center for Humane Technology reads:

We envision a world where Humane Technology is the default for all technology products and services. A combination of new design processes, new goals and metrics, new organizational structures, and new business models would drastically reduce harmful externalities, actively supporting our individual and collective well-being.

This organization believes that the tech companies have a responsibility to consider the human behind the devices and that it's possible to move forward in such a way that we create new technologies without utilizing the "get them hooked" mentality that many companies currently rely upon. This brings us to the convergence of two different types of business: tech companies and the responsibilities that they have and nonprofit organizations that have the potential to raise awareness and create change. Should we limit tech companies in what they can do with their tools? If you agree with the free market and the rights of innovators, then probably not. But perhaps we can encourage the organizations, including the nonprofits, that are doing something about the problem. And this, actually, brings us back to the individuals—because each individual within a company plays a role and has a voice (even though sometimes it doesn't feel like it). Moreover, the individual as a consumer has a lot of power. You can put your money toward the companies that are encouraging addiction, or you can put your money toward the companies that want to create a tech-enriched world that doesn't, as Tristan Harris puts it, downgrade humanity.

Role of Government

What role should the government play in raising awareness about Internet addiction? What about providing funding and support for the people who do develop addiction? And what role, if any, should the government play in regulating the most problematic companies that are aiding in developing addiction? These are murky waters. Government regulation is a divisive topic. But asking the questions is a good starting point.

Author Anya Kamenetz points out something very interesting in her book *The Art of Screen Time*. Back in 1982 (long before smartphones were in our pockets), the National Institutes of Mental Health conducted federally funded research called "Television and Behavior" to determine the effects of those particular screens on our children. What's interesting is that she highlights that this was "the last major piece of federally funded research on children and media." Of course, there has been plenty of other research done by various individuals and institutions. But the quality of the research and its results is always debatable. Perhaps one starting place for the government's role in dealing with Internet addiction would be a federally funded study that's more relevant to our daily lives than the one that took place in 1982. In fact, in 2017, the government started exactly that research. The National Institutes of Health launched a two-year study at the University Study of Connecticut School of Medicine to help determine whether or not Internet addiction is a true disorder. This study looks specifically at gaming, so it doesn't fully address the wider spectrum of Internet addiction risks, but at least it's a starting point. Arguably, the government should play some role in funding this type of research to raise true awareness about the risks of harm, particularly for our society's children.

If the government should be involved in funding research into Internet addiction, should it also be involved in funding treatment? Of course, this gets into the tricky questions associated with government-funded health care. When it comes to substance addiction, there are currently several different ways that the government helps with treatment including through Medicare/Medicaid, Substance Abuse and Mental Health Services Administration grants, specific aid for military veterans, and state-funded addiction treatment centers. Since the government plays a role in funding treatment for drug and alcohol addiction, should the government also help fund treatment for Internet addiction?

Funding is one thing, but what about government regulation? Should the government have laws related to Internet addiction risks? The government regulates intake of addictive substances; some (like heroin) are completely banned, and others (like alcohol) have age and location restrictions. Should there be similar restrictions on certain Internet content? Despite the importance of free speech, we do limit certain types of content, and there are government rules about this. For example, we don't allow child pornography in our society; there are laws against it. But what about how readily children today have access to hard-core pornography featuring adults? There is some regulation in place. In 2000, Congress enacted the Children's Internet Protection Act, which helps to limit the "obscene content" children can view at schools and libraries. In order to receive certain funding, those places must prove that they have an adequate Internet safety policy in place. Can and should the government go further in helping to protect children from this type of content, or is this as far as the government should get involved? From a technology perspective, it would be relatively easy to make it harder for underage people to access hard-core pornography. Whether or not the government should be involved in that is a question up for debate.

In fact, all of this is up for debate. This book is just a starting point for discussion about Internet addiction. We've come up with a basic definition for what Internet addiction is, described the types of content that make people prone to addiction and why that is the case, examined some of the most at-risk populations, looked at different types of treatment options, and reviewed some of the biggest questions and controversies including whether or not we can truly define it as addiction, how widespread the problem is, whether the benefits of technology may outweigh the risks of addiction, and who might be responsible for helping to resolve the addiction problems that do arise. You have a lot of information. Now you can take that forward, dig deeper into your own relationship with technology, and broaden the conversation.

PART III

Scenarios

CHAPTER 12

Case Studies

Case Study 1: Social Media and Texting Addiction

Mariah is a thirteen-year-old girl who lives with her mother and sees her father every other weekend. She's an outgoing, social girl who sometimes gets gently reprimanded by her teachers for talking too much during class. However, overall her teachers like her a lot, and she's always done well in school. She's been on an after-school soccer team for several years. Recently, however, she's getting into more trouble at school, her grades are slipping, and she doesn't want to go to soccer practice. Her parents agree that there's a problem, and they're on the same page about social media and technology being a big part of that problem.

Her parents report that Mariah got her first cell phone when she was ten years old. She also has an iPad and uses the family computer regularly. At first, her parents strictly limited her cell phone use to texting her family members and the close friends that her parents already knew. However, as time went on, she asked for more privileges. Her parents let her set up a Facebook account and an Instagram account, but they have the passwords and would monitor the content regularly.

Over time, they noticed that Mariah was using her phone more and more often. She was constantly on social media. She was also texting all of the time. When Mariah's mom would ask her who she was texting, she would say "Oh, just a friend" but not give any more explanation as to who it was. When her mom would come over to look at the phone screen, she would quickly close the apps she was using. This started to cause a lot of fights with her mother.

At first, her father wasn't as worried as her mom was. He said, "She's a teenager; it's what they do." Mariah's mom takes the phone away at night, so when she found out that her dad was allowing her to be on the phone all night long, she was concerned. They had a co-parenting meeting, in which Mariah's mom expressed that she was worried this behavior was affecting Mariah's sleep and causing her to be more irritable. Mariah's mom explained that her teachers had said she was sassing them, plus she wasn't getting her homework done. Her dad agreed to take the phone away at night. However, the first night that he tried to do so, Mariah threw a tantrum. She was screaming and crying and couldn't seem to control her emotions. Her dad was so overwhelmed that he gave the phone back to her for the night.

He met with Mariah's mother again. They decided that they needed to set up stricter boundaries with Mariah's device use. Plus, they decided that it was time to dig deeper into her texting and social media use. They discovered that she had changed the passwords on her accounts, and they didn't know how to access them. When they eventually got into her social media, they discovered that she had been sending topless photos to boys online. Some of them were in other states, and Mariah had clearly never met them in person, which made her parents worried about who was actually seeing those photos. When her parents tried to talk to her about it, she exploded, screaming about them invading her privacy. At a loss, her parents decided that it was time to seek professional help from a therapist.

Analysis

Mariah is showing several warning signs of Internet addiction. She is using social media and texting more and more often. She is using her phone in the middle of the night, which is compromising her sleep. She doesn't want to engage in extracurricular activities like soccer that she used to love. Although she used to get along well with her teachers and be able to get good grades in school, that's slipping and getting replaced with negative behaviors. All of these are signs that her use of social media could be problematic.

Her secrecy around what she's doing online and the fact that she's been sending risqué photos to people she doesn't know are of particular concern. These are risk-taking behaviors that could pose a significant threat to her real-life safety. They also put her at risk of cyberbullying, so-called revenge porn, catfishing and grooming from online predators, and various problems with her real-life peers. Her parents are right to be concerned.

However, we should be careful not to pathologize Mariah's behavior. Texting, social media use, and beginning to explore her own sexuality are all age-appropriate behaviors. Although her secrecy is concerning, it's normal for young teens to start seeking independence from their parents and to feel upset when their privacy is violated. Despite being of concern, we should recognize the normalcy of these problems among teens Mariah's age today.

Moreover, her therapist not only should take care to consider Internet addiction but also look at other potential issues in Mariah's life before making any diagnosis. Many of Mariah's problems are warning signs of depression—lack of interest in activities, not doing her homework, and mood swings including outbursts. It is possible that Mariah has depression from an unrelated cause and that her misuse of social media is just a symptom of that. It's also possible that she has both depression and Internet addiction, and the two conditions are making each other worse. A therapist should evaluate her completely and neither assume that the Internet is the problem nor avoid addressing that it might be.

It's helpful that her parents are on the same page and are seeking early intervention. They may work together to limit Mariah's use of the Internet. They may opt to take away her cell phone for a period of time, institute stricter rules about when and how she can use it, and/or monitor her activities more vigilantly. They will also want to engage in discussion with her about why they are concerned and what behaviors they would prefer to see. They should also work to address any other underlying issues that arise in therapy. They may wish to supplement Mariah's individual therapy with family counseling to help address both underlying issues and how to negotiate use of social media in their homes.

Case Study 2: Teen Online Gaming Addiction

Sam is a seventeen-year-old gender-fluid individual who uses the pronouns they/them. They began gaming when they were very young. At first, they enjoyed gaming with the family, but soon they became more interested in gaming with friends. Some of their friends from real life also really enjoyed gaming, so when everyone couldn't get together in person, they would meet online in the games instead. Everyone's parents felt like gaming was a supplement to their real-life activities. They noticed benefits for their kids including improved motor skills, better problem-solving abilities, and enhanced ability to work together as a team. All of the friends were in a gaming guild together, and it seemed to strengthen their real-life relationships.

However, over time, things changed for Sam. While the other teens seemed to be able to balance gaming with the rest of their responsibilities at school, activities, and family life, Sam seemed to become obsessed with gaming. They didn't want to get together with their friends in real life anymore; they'd rather just see them in the game. When the gaming guild wasn't online, Sam would game with strangers from the online world. In the last year, Sam has become particularly interested in virtual reality gaming, begging their parents to spend increasing amounts of money on gaming accessories to enhance the virtual reality experience.

Sam's parents are concerned. They've always had a hard time in school. They were diagnosed with attention deficit hyperactivity disorder (ADHD) at age eleven. They were sent home from middle school more than once for aggressive outbursts. Once Sam got into high school, they seemed less aggressive but more withdrawn. Their grades got worse. The only time that they got excited in school was when they were able to do a presentation on the fictional world from the games. That was last year. This year Sam is barely attending classes at all. Their parents can't wake them up to go to school in the mornings, and they're at risk of failing senior year. Sam says that it doesn't matter. They say that school isn't teaching them anything anyway and that they learn a lot more from the Internet than they've ever learned in class.

Although Sam wasn't acting aggressively at school anymore, their aggression at home has increased. Whenever Sam's parents suggest that Sam put their games away and join the family, they resist, and if the parents insist, Sam gets very upset. There are several holes in their bedroom wall due to such incidents. Sam's parents are also increasingly concerned about their health. Sam will sit at the computer for upward of twenty hours at a time, not sleeping and refusing meals. Their parents don't want them to snack on junk food, but it's the only thing they'll eat—quickly, with eyes still on the screen—so sometimes the parents give in. They can't remember the last time that Sam joined them for an activity outside of the house. They're worried about Sam, and they are also frustrated; if Sam doesn't have any plans to finish school or get a job, then will they have to support them forever while they spend all of their time in an online world?

Analysis

Sam appears to be in active addiction with online gaming. This is evidenced by the fact that they're obsessed with gaming to the exclusion of all other activities, that they get angry (which is a withdrawal symptom) when asked to stop gaming, that school performance has gone down as what seems to be a direct result of online gaming, and that there are health concerns including lack of sleep and poor nutrition. At the very least,

Sam does not have a balanced relationship with online gaming and the rest of life.

It's of particular concern that Sam has an ADHD diagnosis. As we saw in Chapter 6, people with ADHD have a greater risk of developing addiction than their peers. Perhaps this is the reason that Sam seemed to become addicted to gaming, whereas their friends are able to control and balance their use. It's sometimes hard to discern cause and effect because Internet addiction can mimic symptoms of ADHD, but because Sam was diagnosed with ADHD when they were young, it's likely that they had ADHD first and have since developed Internet addiction. So, Sam will likely have the dual diagnosis of both mental health disorders: ADHD and Internet addiction. Sam's therapist will have to work with them to determine whether to treat both mental health issues at the same time or address first one and then the other. It will be important to look at the medications Sam is already on for ADHD to get a complete picture.

One potential intervention for Sam could be wilderness camp therapy. This type of therapy would take Sam entirely away from technology for a detox period while also providing them with activities to keep their brain engaged. Wilderness therapy includes both peer support and professional counseling; it will be important to choose a program with counselors who understand both ADHD and Internet addiction. Spending several weeks or months in this type of program might offer Sam the opportunity to build a sense of competence outside of the gaming world, which could foster new outside interests. The slower pace of the natural world compared with that of the gaming world could be very frustrating for Sam at first, but adjusting to that change could help Sam in the long run.

If Sam and their parents choose a wilderness camp, they will also likely want to follow up with individual and/or family therapy. It sounds as if Sam's parents have given up a lot of control in their household. It's age-appropriate for Sam to have a lot of independence, but their parents should still set boundaries. Family therapy could help them establish appropriate boundaries, set new rules around gaming and online activities, and improve their overall family communication so as to heal their fractured relationships.

CASE STUDY 3: INTERNET PORNOGRAPHY ADDICTION

Joseph is a twenty-three-year-old male who lives with his girlfriend who is the same age. They have been dating for about a year and moved in together recently. He is in college and works part-time on campus in a work-study program. He is doing moderately well in school, and there are no complaints from his job. However, he and his girlfriend are fighting a lot recently due to problems associated with his addiction to Internet pornography.

Joseph first started watching porn online when he was a freshman in high school. All of his friends were showing each other different clips and sites. Throughout high school, they continued to share pornography with one another, often one-upping each other to see who could find something more hard-core or unique than the last thing that they saw. Toward the end of high school, though, his friends spent more time focusing on college and relationships with peers. Joseph, on the other hand, turned more and more to Internet pornography.

Whereas it had been easy for him to get aroused when he was younger, it started to take more and more intense scenes to arouse him as he got older. He started venturing into forms of kink that made him feel embarrassed and uncomfortable. He wasn't even sure that he liked these types of scenarios, but nothing else was novel enough to arouse him anymore. He no longer shared his online porn interests with his friends but instead became more and more secretive about it.

When he moved out of his mom's house during his second year of college, he hit rock bottom with his pornography addiction. He started thinking obsessively about porn all of the time. He would spend hours of each day trying to find the perfect clip. He spent less and less time with peers. He struggled in school, and he ended up failing out of the first college that he attended. After failing out, he had to return home. It was then that he admitted to himself, and his mother, that he thought he might have a problem.

Joseph started therapy for a pornography addiction. He did outpatient cognitive behavioral therapy (CBT) to help him better understand what had led him down this path and to resolve the problem. With his permission, his mom was allowed to control the Wi-Fi password, and she would turn the Wi-Fi off except during very limited hours to help him restrict his use. Eventually, he got things under control, and he felt like he was doing well. He got back into a new college program, and he met his current girlfriend.

However, once he and his girlfriend moved in together, things started to backslide. He felt anxious about the relationship. Given the free rein of not being in his mother's house anymore, he started to look at porn online a little bit again to relieve some of that anxiety. When his girlfriend found out, she wasn't upset at first. She figured it was common for people their age to watch porn, and she didn't know about his history of addiction.

However, it quickly became clear that he had a more serious problem. She brought up her concerns that he was watching porn instead of spending time with her.

Joseph immediately recognized that he was having a relapse. Instead of returning to in-person therapy, he joined an online support group for people with an online pornography addiction. He has been able to break the addiction but is now undergoing withdrawal symptoms. He has libido flatline; he can't seem to get an erection at all and doesn't have any interest in having sex with his girlfriend. This is causing a lot of arguments between them. She would like to go to couples' therapy, but he doesn't want to go.

Analysis

Joseph has an online porn addiction, which was diagnosed in therapy in the past, and he has self-diagnosed that he is in a relapse. Some people can watch a little bit of online porn and have no problem, but for Joseph it started to interfere with his entire life. Because he has a history of failing out of school and losing out on peer relationships as a direct result of his addiction, it's important that he take this relapse very seriously. He's currently doing well at work and school and is in a serious relationship that is in jeopardy if he falls further into addiction.

It seems that there were two major triggers for the relapse: leaving the structured environment of his mother's home and dealing with anxiety around his new relationship. He wanted to escape the feelings of anxiety, and perhaps never completely learned how to do that in a healthy way, so he turned to online porn. He was able to do so because there was no structure in place (external or self-imposed) to reduce his access to pornography. It's also problematic that he hadn't revealed his past history of addiction to his girlfriend because she didn't know to help him look out for the warning signs. Plus it points to secrecy in their relationship, which is a risk of Internet addiction.

Online therapy has some potential to help Joseph, and it's good that he's working toward a solution. However, online peer groups vary in quality. Because of his history of addiction, Joseph might be better off returning to in-person therapy. Alternatively, if he prefers online therapy at this time, he might want to look for a licensed counselor, particularly one with training in both CBT and Internet addiction, since CBT did work for him in the past.

It's concerning that he hasn't sought in-person therapy, particularly because his girlfriend would like to try couples' counseling to deal with the problems in their relationship. This suggests that perhaps on some level, Joseph doesn't want to deal head-on with his problems. Maybe he's embarrassed about his porn addiction. Or maybe something else is going on, and he's not ready to address it. For example, it could be that he's not happy in the relationship and doesn't want to stay in it but can't admit that, so he's using his addiction to escape. By not seeking professional help, he's setting himself up for further relapse and subconsciously could want to blame any future relationship failure on the addiction.

Sometimes addiction changes over time. The individual can benefit from not only relearning their coping skills but also digging deeper to gain further insight into their addiction. Joseph may find that talk therapy is helpful for that. On the other hand, if he decides to keep treating himself through peer support online, he might at least want to implement a structured method of contemplative computing or some form of digital diet to help him in daily life.

CASE STUDY 4: ADULT ONLINE GAMING ADDICTION

Matthew is a thirty-three-year-old father of two young children. He has been married to their mother for almost ten years. They used to have a great relationship, but after the children came along, they seemed to grow apart. Matthew feels that she focused all of her attention on them, and it made him feel lonely and unvalued in his home. In the past few years, whenever he's home, he spends all of his time on online gaming.

Matthew had always enjoyed gaming when he was younger and never had any problems with it. He would sometimes lose track of time because he would get so immersed in a game, but it never presented any serious issues in his life. When he got married, he stopped gaming so much because he and his wife would do other things with their downtime such as go to movies together and throw parties with friends. Once he started finding himself bored at home, it made sense to him to return to online gaming. He enjoys coming home from work, heading to the computer, and relaxing in that online world.

His wife is not happy with this situation. Her perspective is that he doesn't want to spend any time with her and the kids. He would rather have fun in the online gaming world than sit down to a family dinner or help the kids with bath time and bedtime. She feels completely disconnected from him. When she tries to talk to him about it, he gets upset. He says, "I go to work and earn the money for this family. I'm not out at a bar or with other women. I'm right here in the house. So, what if I want to chill out with my game?" Matthew's online friends agree with his perspective and say that his wife is nagging him too much.

Recently, Matthew's wife has been considering getting a divorce. She had hoped that the problem would pass, but it seems like it's getting worse. Recently, her youngest son walked over to his dad when Matthew was gaming because he wanted to ask his dad to read a book to him. Matthew didn't even hear what the child was saying, and his son got very upset at being ignored. He threw a tantrum, and his mother was unable to make him feel better for nearly an hour. Another recent problem was that their oldest son tried gaming with their dad. She had concerns about her young child playing violent video games but thought that at least it could be a way for him to bond with his father. Unfortunately, Matthew got really upset because his young son couldn't keep up in the game and made him lose out on some points that he wanted to acquire. He exploded, his son ended up in tears, and Matthew went back to his game alone. At her wits' end, Matthew's wife is starting to think it would be better if he weren't there at all.

Analysis

It's hard to say whether or not Matthew has a full-blown gaming addiction. He's never had a problem with it before now. He's able to hold down a job, and gaming doesn't interfere with his finances. He hasn't noted any particular health symptoms associated with gaming. In fact, he doesn't think that there's a problem at all. But it's of great concern that he seems to be increasingly distant from his family, even to the point of blowing up at his young son for "losing" a game, and that's one warning sign that there's a problem. It might not qualify as an addiction, but it also might be one.

An addiction often develops when a person wants to escape uncomfortable feelings. It sounds as though that's exactly what Matthew has been doing—trying to escape the discomfort in his family that developed after the birth of his children. Something about being a father makes him feel incompetent and unneeded, and perhaps gaming offers him not just an escape but a place where he feels like he's competent at something. He excels at online gaming, and he has peer support there, whereas at home it just feels like he's doing everything wrong.

The gaming seems to be making the problem at home worse. Ironically, although he thinks that his family doesn't need him and that he's useless there, his family is actually very clearly making bids for his attention. They want him engaged with their daily activities, like reading a book to the kids at bedtime, but he's so immersed in his game that he can't seem to see that. Perhaps this is because he has an addiction and is blind to their bids. Perhaps he feels like if he tried to participate in family time, it would just be a fight, so he turns to gaming instead. Either way, the family is in trouble.

If Matthew wants to resolve the problems at home, then he might benefit from seeking individual or family counseling. These are two very different approaches to the problem, and he would have to determine which is best for him. Since he doesn't feel like online gaming is a problem, he wouldn't likely seek therapy specifically for Internet addiction. However, he could get therapeutic help to deal with his family issues. He recognizes that there's a problem there, and talking to a professional—alone or with his family—could help him deal with those underlying issues. If it turns out that there's a true Internet addiction, that might arise later in therapy and could be dealt with in turn. It may instead be the case that resolving his family issues naturally causes him to turn to gaming less frequently.

CASE STUDY 5: ONLINE SHOPPING ADDICTION

Marni is a fifty-three-year-old woman who lives at home alone. She has three children, the youngest of whom just left for college last year. She had been a stay-at-home mom when her children were young, and that was the best time of her life. She loved caring for them, baking with them, making costumes for Halloween, and participating in their school activities. As they got older, they needed her less, so she went back to work part-time. Her husband, who had supported the family, asked for a divorce when the youngest children were in high school. At that time, she had to get a full-time job. She started doing administrative work at an office, and she's competent at it but doesn't enjoy it at all.

Marni doesn't really know what to do with herself now that her kids have all left the home. She works in order to pay her bills, but she doesn't derive any satisfaction from the work. She longs for the old days when her house was filled with noise and laughter. She's always asking her kids to come home on their school breaks, and she's thrilled when they do. She can't wait until they start having kids of their own so that she can be a grandma. But in the meantime, she's just passing the time.

When she gets home from work, she immediately turns on the television for background noise. Then she starts browsing online. Since she works full-time now, she never feels like going out to the store, so she does all of her shopping online. It started out with just getting her groceries delivered once a week. She discovered that she really enjoyed browsing those online aisles, putting new foods in her cart that she never noticed at the grocery store. She loves that moment when the delivery person arrives, and she exchanges a quick hello and then gets to unpack everything she ordered.

In fact, she loves it so much that she started doing a lot of other online shopping as well. She visits Amazon almost every day to see what new items she might need for her home. She's even started stockpiling items for her grandbabies, despite the fact that none of her children are ready to have kids yet. She loves picking out just the right thing and gets excited again when it arrives at her doorstep. Sometimes she even forgets what she ordered, so it's particularly thrilling to get those little surprises in the mail.

Unfortunately, all of that shopping has added up. Marni has nearly maxed out all of her credit cards. She received the house in the divorce, and she has refinanced in it in order to cover her debts. She is thinking about digging into her retirement accounts because she needs more money. Despite hating her job, she's been working overtime to help cover the costs of shopping online. Her children do not know that she's in this situation.

Marni has friends who would like to spend time with her. However, she always tells them that she doesn't have the money to go out. Recently, they've been making less of an effort to see her. When she's not shopping online, she's usually streaming television shows and simultaneously playing simple games, such as Farmville, on her phone. She doesn't like that she spends her time that way but figures it's better than spending money shopping. Inevitably, though, she always heads back to that Amazon button to see if there's something new there that she "needs."

Analysis

Marni has an Internet addiction that is primarily focused on online shopping. However, when she's able to restrict herself from online shopping, it does manifest in addiction to other forms of content such as simple games. This suggests that when she tries not to shop online, she experiences feelings of withdrawal, which is a huge red flag that she's got an addiction. In order to quell the withdrawal, she turns to other online activities to soothe herself.

Her use has grown over time. She has stopped seeing her friends, claiming that she doesn't have the money to go out but then spending that money shopping online instead. She is able to hold down her job, so the addiction hasn't hindered her in that way, yet. However, she's in serious debt due specifically to her online addiction. It's compromised her future in that she's refinanced her home and might use her retirement income to pay for her addiction. These are all serious problems that seem to only be growing with time. She has not admitted her problem to anyone else; keeping it a secret is another sign of addiction.

Marni seems to have developed this addiction specifically because of her change in life circumstances. Her husband left, and her children moved out on their own. Her identity as a mother, the experience of which gave her great joy, has changed. Having not fully processed that loss in a healthy way, Marni seems to be trying to escape those uncomfortable feelings of grief through her addiction. A therapist should assess Marni for depression, as it is possible that her grief turned into depression and that triggered the addiction. Marni likely gets a pleasant "feel good" hit of dopamine each time she puts something into her online shopping cart and again when it arrives at her doorstep. She's trying to feel good more and more by engaging more and more in that behavior.

Most likely, dealing with the underlying emotional issues will help Marni in reducing her compulsion to shop online. However, because it's become such an addictive activity, she and her therapist might want to address that issue directly as well. They may want to put a plan in place to help restrict her from online shopping while simultaneously dealing with the underlying issues of loss, change in identity, depression, and so forth. Hopefully, over time, Marni will find new ways of spending her time rather than shopping online. Perhaps she'll get a job she actually likes or begin spending time out of the house with friends.

GLOSSARY

Addiction: The need to engage in a behavior or use a substance despite negative life consequences, often increasing the duration and intensity of use over time and experiencing withdrawal when trying to quit.

ADHD: Attention deficit hyperactivity disorder is a mental health issue characterized by problems with attention and impulsivity.

Adrenaline: A hormone in the body that we secrete when we feel stress, also called the fight-or-flight hormone.

Affective Forecasting Error: A tendency in the brain to incorrectly assume that something that gave us pleasure before will give us pleasure again.

Amygdala: A part of the brain related directly to how we experience emotions.

Anxiety: Excessive worry and fear, which you are unable to control, and which causes you distress.

ASD: Autism spectrum disorders, with symptoms that include trouble with communication and social interaction as well as a narrow range of interests and/or behaviors including repetitive moments.

Attention Restoration Theory: An idea first posited in the 1980s by Rachel and Stephen Kaplan that spending downtime in nature has a restorative effect that helps humans to heal.

Augmented Reality: When you view the real world through a screen, such as a cell phone, and see something on the screen that isn't there in real life.

Body Dysmorphic Disorder: Mental health condition in which the person obsesses over their flaws, grooms and exercises excessively, avoids mirrors, constantly works to change their appearance, and has negative self-esteem.

Bottom-up Attention: When something attracts us and demands that we notice it, so we don't control where our focus goes.

Catfishing: The act of pretending to be someone else online in order to lure one or more people into a relationship with your fake persona.

Causation: Proof that one thing happens as a direct result of another; in contrast to correlation.

CBT: Cognitive behavioral therapy, a form of therapy that uses goal-oriented problem-solving to help people change their patterns of both thought and behavior.

Cellular Neuroplasticity: A change in the number of brain cells that are talking to each other.

CIAS: Chen Internet Addiction Scale, a tool used to measure Internet addiction in Chinese adolescents.

Circadian Rhythm: Physical and mental patterns that we follow each day, related to our experience of the changing sunlight, and directly related to our sleep cycle.

Classical Conditioning: How we learn to respond to one thing when two items are paired together even after the second item is removed from the equation.

Comorbidity: When one person has two or more diagnoses for different mental health disorders, one of which is usually an addiction; also called dual diagnosis or co-occurring disorders.

Compulsive Behavior: Repeatedly engaging in a specific action whether or not you get any satisfaction from doing so.

Contemplative Computing: Mindfulness approach to limiting Internet use in order to maximize the benefits and minimize the addictive harms.

Correlation: Indications that two phenomena are linked but not necessarily that one happens as a result of the other; in contrast to causation.

Cortisol: A stress hormone in the body.

Cyberbullying: Persistent bullying of one or more people that takes place through apps, text, and social media.

Cyberchondria: A form of hypochondria directly related to the tendency to search online for information about potential medical conditions, becoming increasingly certain that you're deathly ill because of what the Internet has to say.

Dating App Addiction: Using apps such as Tinder or Hinge with increasing frequency even though the rewards that you get from it are diminishing and/or there are negative consequences in other areas of your life.

Depersonalization: The feeling that you are not a real person.

Depression: Feelings of low mood and lack of interest in things that you previously enjoyed as well as other physical and mental health symptoms.

Derealization: An inability to know what is real.

Desensitization: Diminished emotional response to something after being exposed to it multiple times.

Digital Diet: Reducing or eliminating use of some or all Internet devices and activities to help break an Internet addiction; also called a digital fast.

Disconnectivity Anxiety: Feelings of fear, stress, anger, and frustration caused by the unexpected inability to connect to your phone or the Internet.

Dopamine: A neurotransmitter in the brain often called the "feel good chemical."

DSM: *Diagnostic and Statistical Manual of Mental Disorders*, a guide used by psychologists and other health-care professionals in the United States to officially diagnose all mental disorders.

Email Apnea: A tendency to hold your breath or breathe more shallowly when opening email, checking social media comments, and so forth.

Euphoric Recall: A tendency to remember positive feelings associated with a behavior or event while forgetting the negative feelings.

Exposure and Response Prevention: A form of CBT for treatment of phobias and some other disorders in which the person is exposed to the source of their fear and learns to modulate their response.

FOMO: Fear of missing out, the feeling that other people are online doing something interesting and that if you fail to get online as well, then you're going to be excluded from the fun.

Frontal Lobe: Part of the brain that helps us with "higher-level" functioning such as problem-solving, planning, and regulating our emotions.

GABA: Gamma-aminobutyric acid, neurotransmitter related to stress reduction.

Game Transfer Phenomenon: Short-term psychosis that causes a gaming player to have trouble separating the game from reality.

Gaming Addiction: Playing video/Internet games with increasing frequency even though the rewards that you get from it are diminishing and/or there are negative consequences in other areas of your life.

General Internet Addiction: Problematic Internet use including withdrawal, tolerance, and continued use despite negative consequences—with no particular content focus but instead to the compulsive use of being online.

Gray Matter: The bulk of what we see when we look at a human brain—the wrinkled, pinkish-gray tissue consisting of cell bodies, dendrites, and nerve synapses.

Grounding: Therapeutic techniques to help people to come into the present moment by focusing on their senses.

Harm Reduction: An approach to treating addiction in which the goal isn't abstinence but rather reducing the damages of use.

Hippocampus: Part of the brain related to learning and forming memories.

HPA Axis: Hypothalamic pituitary adrenal axis, a combination of interacting parts of the brain that relate to our stress responses.

Hyperarousal: An increase in physical and psychological response to stimuli, which might include being abnormally alert to danger and having a racing heart.

Hypochondria: Extreme anxiety about one's health, often imagining that you have an illness that isn't there.

ICD: *International Classification of Diseases*, a system maintained by the World Health Organization (WHO) to classify all different types of health issues, including those related to mental health.

Imposter Syndrome: The belief that you are a fraud and other people are eventually going to find out the truth about you.

Intermittent Rewards: When we sometimes receive pleasure, but sometimes don't, from the same activity or trigger; also called variable-ratio reward schedule.

Mesocortical Pathway: Dopamine pathway in the brain linked with cognitive and emotional abilities as well as memory, attention, and our ability to learn.

Mesolimbic Pathway: Dopamine pathway in the brain linked with seeking pleasure and reward.

Mindfulness: The practice of focusing on being entirely present in the moment.

MMORPG: Massive multiplayer online role-playing games, in which thousands or sometimes millions of people around the world participate in the game at the same time, playing in a virtual scenario.

Myelin: An insulating layer that wraps around the white matter in the brain, protecting the axons and solidifying their function.

Net Compulsions: Variety of activities that addicts engage in repeatedly and obsessively including online gambling, auction bidding, and stock trading.

Neuroplasticity: The brain's ability to change and grow over time; also called brain plasticity or neuroelasticity.

Neurotransmitters: The communicators, or messengers, in the brain that transmit information from one area to another.

Nigrostriatal Pathway: Dopamine pathway in the brain linked with movement and sensory stimulation.

Norepinephrine: Neurotransmitter related to the fight-or-flight instinct.

Nucleus Accumbens: A cluster of nerve cells often called the "brain's pleasure center."

Online Pornography Addiction: Accessing pornographic websites and/or apps with increasing frequency even though the rewards that you get from it are diminishing and/or there are negative consequences in other areas of your life.

Phantom Vibration Syndrome: Imagining that you feel the vibration of a phone alert when the phone isn't even on you.

Prefrontal Cortex: The front part of the frontal lobe in the brain, responsible for higher-order functions like attention, planning, prioritizing, impulse control behavior, emotional control, and adjusting to complicated and varying situations.

Psychosis: A mental disorder in which you lose contact with what is real.

PTSD: Posttraumatic stress disorder, a mental health condition that can occur after many different types of trauma and includes symptoms such as intrusive thoughts, flashbacks, and panic.

Sedentary Lifestyle: Spending most or all of your time either sitting or lying down rather than engaging in physical activity.

Selfie Addiction: Taking, editing, and posting photos of yourself with increasing frequency even though the rewards that you get from it are diminishing and/or there are negative consequences in other areas of your life.

Serotonin: Neurotransmitter related to mood stabilization.

Social Media Addiction: Using sites such as Facebook and Instagram with increasing frequency even though the rewards that you get from it are diminishing and/or there are negative consequences in other areas of your life.

Social Phobia: Anxiety related to social settings, which can include being in groups and speaking in public.

Specific Internet Addiction: Problematic Internet use including withdrawal, tolerance, and continued use despite negative consequences—with focus on one or more very specific types of content such as gaming, gambling, social media, or pornography.

Switchtasking: Moving our focus from one thing to the other and back again, which is what we're usually doing when we think that we are multitasking.

Synaptic Neuroplasticity: A change in the strength of the connection across the junction from one brain cell to the next.

Text Neck: Chronic pain associated with damage to the spine done because of poor posture when spending excessive amounts of time on a cell phone.

Texting Addiction: Using text apps and direct-to-one-person chat tools with increasing frequency even though the rewards that you get from it are diminishing and/or there are negative consequences in other areas of your life.

Texting Thumb: Repetitive stress injury that typically results in pain at the base of thumb due to excessive smartphone use.

Tolerance: Adapting to an addiction so that you need more of the behavior or substance in order to achieve the same feelings.

Top-Down Attention: When we set goals and direct where our attention will go in order to meet those goals.

Trolling: Purposely posting inflammatory comments online in order to get a group riled up and engaging negatively.

Ventral-Tegmental Area: Part of the brain rich in dopamine and related to our desire for rewards.

Virtual Reality: When you look at a screen (usually through glasses or headsets) and immerse yourself entirely into the world there, sometimes with additional sensory input from haptics to make it feel even more like you're in that world.

Voyeurism: Taking pleasure in watching someone else, particularly when they're doing something private, dangerous, or scandalous.

White Matter: Bundles of axons that connect gray matter areas in the brain.

Withdrawal: Physical and mental symptoms that appear when trying to quit an addiction.

TIMELINE

1994	Kimberly Young begins a three-year study into the emerging issue of Internet addiction. The results are published in a book titled *Caught in the Net*.
1995	Kimberly Young founds the Center for Internet Addiction.
1995	Match.com launches the first-ever commercial dating website.
March 8, 1995	*The New York Times* publishes an article titled "The Lure and Addiction of Life OnLine." This is likely the first time that the term "Internet addiction" is used in a major publication.
Late 1990s	Scientists begin identifying the traits of Internet addiction using criteria from substance and behavior addiction.
Late 1990s	Pacific Quest opens in Hawaii as a wilderness therapy program for teenagers; it will eventually come to focus on Internet addiction treatment.
2001	An Indiana School of Medicine study finds that the brain changes after just one week of playing violent video games.
2003	Mary Christina Cordell and her boyfriend are so focused on playing the online game *EverQuest* that they forget their child in the car and the child dies. The media suggests that gaming addiction is the cause of death.
2004	Facebook launches.
2004	*World of Warcraft* launches. In its first ten years, the game gained more than one hundred million subscribers around the world. It received $10 billion in gross income. It is considered one of the most highly addictive online games available.

2004	The first Internet addiction treatment center opens, in Beijing, China. It is a military-style boot camp.
2007	Apple releases the first iPhone, and soon smartphone use becomes ubiquitous.
2007	Jarice Hanson authors the book *24/7: How Cell Phones and the Internet Change the Way We Live, Work, and Play*. This is one of the earliest books on the potential negative harms of our modern use of the Internet.
2008	Chinese Ministry of Health approves a manual addressing Internet addiction disorder and naming it a number one health crisis.
2009	Facebook introduces the addictive "like" button.
2009	Dr. Dean Fisherman opens the Text Neck Institute to treat chronic pain associated with excessive phone use.
2009	reSTART opens. It is the first residential treatment center in the United States for people struggling with Internet addiction.
2010	Instagram launches.
2011	*Israel Journal of Psychiatry and Related Sciences* publishes a study from Tel Aviv University of the first documented cases of Internet-related psychosis.
2012	Larry Rosen authors the book *iDisorder*, in which he suggests we are all increasingly showing symptoms of common mental health issues due to the ubiquity of smartphone and computer use.
2013	Alex Soojung-Kim Pang authors the book *The Distraction Addiction*. He coins the term "contemplative computing" to describe mindful practices of using the Internet while avoiding its addictive nature.
2013	Psious is founded. This is a virtual reality company that uses technology to help treat mental health issues.
February 2013	Tristan Harris of Google releases an internal presentation called "A Call to Minimize Distraction & Respect Users' Attention." It criticizes how major tech companies are exploiting the brain's addictive tendencies in order to grow their bottom line.
May 2013	The American Psychiatric Association releases the *DSM*-5. For the first time, it includes online gaming addiction as an area suggested for further study.
2014	*American Psychologist* publishes research into the benefits of online gaming for children, suggesting that there are both positives and negatives to frequent Internet use.

2014	A study called Facebook's Emotional Consequences finds that social media can cause depression.
2014	Nir Eyal authors the book *Hooked: How to Build Habit-Forming Products*, which others go on to use in their research into Internet addiction.
2015	Tristan Harris, who previously criticized Google's exploitation of users' tendencies toward addiction, leaves his job at Google. He founds the Time Well Spent project and the Center for Humane Technology.
2015	Mai-Ly Steers conducts a study at University of Houston that specifically finds that Facebook use increases the frequency of users comparing themselves to others, which in turn leads to depression.
2015	Dr. Kelly Lister-Landman completes a study into compulsive text messaging among adolescents that finds that girls experience negative consequences at much higher rate than boys.
2016	Nicholas Kardaras authors the book *Glow Kids: How Screen Addiction Is Hijacking Our Kids—and How to Break the Trance*.
June 2016	*Computer Methods and Programs in Biomedicine* publishes research suggesting that virtual reality can help in the treatment of online gaming addiction.
July 6, 2016	*Pokemon Go* launches on smartphones as the first highly popular augmented reality video game.
October 2016	Virtual reality company Limbix is founded. It uses technology to aid in mental health treatment.
2017	The National Institutes of Health launches a two-year study at the University of Connecticut School of Medicine to help determine whether or not Internet addiction is a true disorder.
2017	An episode of *Real Time* airs in which Bill Maher compares "the tycoons of social media" to tobacco farmers, exploiting our tendency toward addiction.
2017	Psychologists Mark Griffiths and Daria Kuss of Nottingham Trent University publish a paper analyzing the specific addictive nature of social media.
2017	VICE reports on a Match.com study that finds that one out of six single people feels addicted to the process of seeking out a partner online.
2017	A study by Yale University finds that teens on the autism spectrum reported better quality friendships when they

	utilized social media to aid in communication. This suggests that there are both benefits and harms to Internet use for certain populations.
2017	Adam Alter authors the book *Irresistible: The Rise of Addictive Technology and the Business of Keeping Us Hooked.*
2018	The movie *Ready Player One* hits theaters. It explores the benefits of living in a virtual world but makes an argument that it's also valuable to live in "real reality."
September 17, 2018	Apple releases iOS 12, which includes the new Screen Time feature to help users monitor and limit their smartphone usage.
May 2019	The World Health Organization publishes *ICD*-11. For the first time, it names online gaming as a specific health disorder. The criteria it offers for diagnosing this issue go into full effect in 2022.

Sources for Further Information

Books

Aarons-Mele, Morra. 2017. *Hiding in the Bathroom: An Introvert's Roadmap to Getting Out There (When You'd Rather Stay Home)*. New York: Dey Street Books.

Alter, Adam. 2017. *Irresistible: The Rise of Addictive Technology and the Business of Keeping Us Hooked*. New York: Penguin Press.

Caspar, George. 2014. *Shame and Internet Trolling: A Personal Exploration of the Mindset behind This Modern Behavior*. BookBaby.

Eyal, Nir. 2014. *Hooked: How to Build Habit-Forming Products*. New York: Portfolio.

Goldstein, Meredith. *I Can't Help Myself: Lessons and Confessions from a Modern Advice Columnist*. New York: Grand Central Publishing.

Gurdon, Meghan C. 2019. *The Enchanted Hour: The Miraculous Power of Reading Aloud in the Age of Distraction*. New York: HarperCollins.

Hanson, Jarice. 2007. *24/7: How Cell Phones and the Internet Change the Way We Live, Work, and Play*. Westport, CT: Praeger.

Hari, Johann. 2018. *Lost Connections: Uncovering the Real Causes of Depression—and the Unexpected Solutions*. New York: Bloomsbury.

James, Laura. 2018. *Odd Girl Out: My Extraordinary Autistic Life*. Berkeley: Seal Press.

Kamenetz, Anya. 2018. *The Art of Screen Time: How Your Family Can Balance Digital Media and Real Life*. New York: PublicAffairs.

Kardaras, Nicholas. 2016. *Glow Kids: How Screen Addiction Is Hijacking Our Kids—and How to Break the Trance*. New York: St. Martin's Press.

Kuss, Daria J., and Griffiths, Mark D. 2014. *Internet Addiction in Psychotherapy*. London: Palgrave.

Newport, Cal. 2019. *Digital Minimalism: Choosing a Focused Life in a Noisy World*. New York: Portfolio.

Pang, Alex S.-K. 2013. *The Distraction Addiction: Getting the Information You Need and the Communication You Want without Enraging Your Family, Annoying Your Colleagues, and Destroying Your Soul*. New York: Little, Brown and Company.

Pierce, Jennifer B. 2017. *Sex, Brains, and Video Games: Information and Inspiration for Youth Services Librarians*. 2nd ed. Chicago: ALA Editions, an imprint of the American Library Association.

Richtel, Matt. 2014. *A Deadly Wandering: A Mystery, a Landmark Investigation, and the Astonishing Science of Attention in the Digital Age*. New York: William Morrow/HarperCollins.

Roberts, Kevin. 2010. *Cyber Junkie: Escaping the Gaming and Internet Trap*. Center City, MN: Hazelden.

Rosen, Larry. 2012. *iDisorder*. New York: Palgrave Macmillan.

Sieberg, Daniel. 2011. *The Digital Diet: The 4-Step Plan to Break Your Tech Addiction and Regain Balance in Your Life*. New York: Harmony.

Surratt, Carla. 1999. *Netaholics? The Creation of a Pathology*. Commack, NY: Nova Science Publishers.

Turkle, Sherry. 2012. *Alone Together: Why We Expect More from Technology and Less from Each Other*. New York: Basic Books.

Young, Kimberly S. 1998. *Caught in the Net: How to Recognize the Signs of Internet Addiction—and a Winning Strategy for Recovery*. New York: Wiley.

ARTICLES

Austin, Darren. 2017. "I Bought an Amazon Echo Last Year—and Now I Can't Imagine Life without It." Business Insider. June 29. https://www.businessinsider.com/hooked-model-explains-why-amazon-alexa-is-so-addictive-2017-6.

Campbell-Meiklejohn, Daniel et al. 2010. "Serotonin and Dopamine Play Complementary Roles in Gambling to Recover Losses." *Neuropsychopharmacology*. October 27. https://www.nature.com/articles/npp2010170.

Dold, Kristen. 2017. "Dating App Addiction Is Real." Vice. February 10. https://www.vice.com/en_us/article/qkxdkv/dating-app-addiction-is-real.

Gottberg, Kathy. "Is My Husband in Love with Alexa or Is She Only a Temporary Distraction?" SMARTLiving365.com. https://www.smartliving365.com/is-my-husband-in-love-with-alexa-or-is-she-only-a-temporary-distraction/.

Lister-Landman, Kelly M., and Domoff, Sarah E. 2015. "The Role of Compulsive Texting in Adolescents' Academic Functioning." American Psychological Association. Retrieved from https://www.apa.org/pubs/journals/releases/ppm-ppm0000100.pdf.

Mendhekar, Dattatreya N., and Andrade C. Chittaranjan. 2012. "Emergence of Psychotic Symptoms during Internet Withdrawal." *Psychiatry and Clinical*

Neurosciences. February 12. https://onlinelibrary.wiley.com/doi/full/10.1111/j.1440-1819.2011.02306.x.

Mosher, Dave. 2011. "High Wired: Does Addictive Internet Use Restructure the Brain?" *Scientific American.* June 17. Retrieved from https://www.scientificamerican.com/article/does-addictive-internet-use-restructure-brain/.

Newman, Tim. 2018. "Anxiety in the West: Is It on the Rise?" *Medical News Today.* September 5. https://www.medicalnewstoday.com/articles/322877.php.

O'Neill, M. 1995. "The Lure and Addiction of Life OnLine." *The New York Times.* https://www.nytimes.com/1995/03/08/garden/the-lure-and-addiction-of-life-on-line.html.

Park, Sung Yong et al. 2016. "The Effects of a Virtual Reality Treatment Program for Online Gaming Addiction." *Computer Methods and Programs in Biomedicine.* June. https://www.sciencedirect.com/science/article/pii/S0169260716000079.

Pelley, Virginia. 2017. "Can You Get Addicted to Trolling?" Vice. September 6. https://www.vice.com/en_us/article/a33yq8/trolling-addiction.

Ryan, Richard et al. 2006. "The Motivational Pull of Video Games: A Self-Determination Theory Approach." *Motivation and Emotion.* Springer Science + Business Media. https://selfdeterminationtheory.org/SDT/documents/2006_RyanRigbyPrzybylski_MandE.pdf.

Sagioglou, Christina, and Tobias Greitemeyer. 2014. "Facebook's Emotional Consequences: Why Facebook Causes a Decrease in Mood and Why People Still Use It." *Computers in Human Behavior.* https://www.researchgate.net/publication/261563413_Facebook's_emotional_consequences_Why_Facebook_causes_a_decrease_in_mood_and_why_people_still_use_it.

Snodgrass, Jeffrey et al. 2011. "Magical Flight and Monstrous Stress: Technologies of Absorption and Mental Wellness in Azeroth." *Culture, Medicine and Psychiatry.* https://www.researchgate.net/publication/49690512_Magical_Flight_and_Monstrous_Stress_Technologies_of_Absorption_and_Mental_Wellness_in_Azeroth.

Steers, Mai-Ly. 2014. "Seeing Everyone Else's Highlight Reels: How Facebook Usage Is Linked to Depressive Symptoms." *Journal of Social and Clinical Psychology.* October. https://guilfordjournals.com/doi/abs/10.1521/jscp.2014.33.8.701.

Van Schalkwyk, Gerrit et al. 2017. "Yale Study: Social Media Boosts Friendship Quality in Adolescents with Autism Spectrum Disorder." Yale Child Study Center. June 19. https://medicine.yale.edu/childstudy/news/article.aspx?id=15234.

Ward, D. M. et al. 2018. "Social Media Use and Happiness in Adults with Autism Spectrum Disorder." *Cyberpsychology, Behavior and Social Networking.* March. https://www.ncbi.nlm.nih.gov/pubmed/29485900.

West, Darrell M., and John R. Allen. 2018. "How Artificial Intelligence Is Transforming the World." Brookings. April 24. https://www.brookings.edu/research/how-artificial-intelligence-is-transforming-the-world/.

TREATMENT PROGRAMS

Behavioral Health of the Palm Beaches. https://www.bhpalmbeach.com.
blueFire Wilderness Therapy. https://bluefirewilderness.com.
The Center for Internet and Technology Addiction. https://virtual-addiction.com.
Computer Addiction Services. http://www.computeraddiction.com.
The Computer Addiction Treatment Program. https://www.computeraddiction
     treatment.com.
Illinois Institute for Addiction Recovery. http://www.addictionrecov.org.
Life Process Program from Porn Addiction Recovery. https://lifeprocessprogram
     .com/porn-addiction/.
Outback Therapeutic Expeditions. https://www.outbacktreatment.com.
Pacific Quest. https://pacificquest.org.
reSTART. https://www.netaddictionrecovery.com.

ADDITIONAL ONLINE RESOURCES

Center for Humane Technology. https://humanetech.com
Internet Addiction Test Kit for Families. https://www.stoeltingco.com/internet-
     addiction-test-kit-iat-kit.html.
On-Line Gamers Anonymous. https://www.olganon.org/home.
Pornography Addicts Anonymous. https://www.pornaddictsanonymous.org.
Time to Log Off. https://www.itstimetologoff.com.
Wowaholics Anonymous. http://www.wowaholics.org.

INDEX

184

mental health and substance
abuse issues, 90–91; socially
isolated individuals, 89–90;
susceptibility traits, 92
Attention deficit hyperactivity disorder
(ADHD): at-risk addiction of
individuals with, 86–87; case
study of teen online gaming
addiction, 160–61; dual
diagnosis and, 116
Attention engineering, 49
Attention Restoration Theory, 85
Auctions, online, 76
Augmented reality, 137; virtual reality
and, 138–43
Austin, Darren, 144
Autism spectrum disorders (ASD),
117; at-risk addiction of
individuals with, 87–89; benefits
of Internet for, 123–25

Baby boomers, 6
Bailenson, Jeremy, 140
Bean, Mary A., 122
Behavioral Health of the Palm
Beaches, Inc., 97
Benefits of Internet, 121–22; accessing
therapy online, 129–31; for
autism spectrum disorders
(ASDs), 123–25; for education,
131–33; for online gaming,
127–29; for people feeling
isolated, 125–27; for solving
Internet addiction, 133–35
Big Tobacco, 50
Binge watching, Netflix and,
76–78
Biopsychosocial model, social media
addiction, 56
Bipolar mania, 24
BlackBerry, 137
Blackberry thumb, 28
Black Mirror (television/Netflix), 151
BlueFire, 99
Body dysmorphic disorder, 57

Brain: addiction in, 39–40; cortisol
and, 26, 28, 72; dopamine
and reward system of, 40–44;
frontal lobe and prefrontal
cortex of, 45–46, 84; gamma-
aminobutyric acid (GABA)
in, 44; gray matter and white
matter in, 46–47; growth and
development of young children,
85; neuroplasticity of, 47–48,
84; neurotransmitters of, 40–45,
72; norepinephrine in, 44–45;
nucleus accumbens of, 40, 43;
serotonin in, 43–44; stimulation
with gaming, 72; susceptibility
of, 48–51; teenager's, 84–85
Bullying. See Cyberbullying
Businesses, role of, in Internet
addiction, 152–53
Business Insider, 144

Caffeine, 109–10
CAGE questionnaire, 12
California State University (CSU), 91
Call of Duty (game), 89
Carpal tunnel syndrome, 27
Case studies: adult online gaming
addiction, 164–66; Internet
pornography addiction, 161–64;
online shopping addiction,
166–68; social media and texting
addiction, 157–59; teen online
gaming addiction, 159–61
Case Western Reserve University
School of Medicine, 117
Caspar, George, 64
Catfish (television show), 63
Catfishing, 62–63
Caught in the Net (Young), 7
Causation, 107, 108
Cause and effect, 107, 110
Cell phone adoption, 17
Center for Humane Technology, 152
Center for Internet Addiction, 18
Centers for Disease Control, 30

About the Author

Kathryn Vercillo is a full-time writer with a master's degree in psychological studies. She is passionate about mental health topics and helping to raise awareness about these issues in ways that destigmatize them while offering inspiration and help to those in need. She loves technology but feels that it needs to be balanced with analog activities that connect mind-heart-body. Some of her previous books are *Crochet Saved My Life* and *Hook to Heal*, which explore the possibilities of handcrafting for dealing with mental and physical health issues. When not writing or crocheting, she enjoys long walks with her rescue dog, deep talks with her family and friends, and partaking of the creativity that her San Francisco home has to offer.